FAITH IN REAL ESTATE

BY TRICIA ANDREASSEN

CO-AUTHORED BY:
DIRK ZELLER

RICKY CAIN

MELISSA CARPENTER

JEN MAINS

J. MICHAEL MANLEY

AMANDA POWELL

KELLIE RUTHERFORD

ANGELA THOMPSON

Creative Life
Publishing & Learning
INSTITUTE

Creative Life Publishing & Learning Institute
www.CLPLI.com
Info@CLPLI.com

Book Versions
Ingram ISBN: 978-1-946265-27-2
eBook ISBN: 978-1-946265-28-9
KDP Paperback ISBN: 978-1-946265-29-6

Cover Design and Layout by Dara Rogers

CONTENTS

✝

Chapter 1
A Voice to Stand in Faith–Together

BY TRICIA ANDREASSEN

In recent years, I have known too many people who were in real estate who have tragically taken their lives. These people were perceived as successful according to the standards of quantifiable means such as: how many transactions they did, how many team members they led, how many times they were asked to speak at a real estate conference or contribute to real estate education. But with all that success, something just wasn't right.

Perhaps they felt overwhelmed. Maybe they felt like they were a failure no matter how much they accomplished. It could be that the financial burden coupled with the feeling of needed success smothered them.

What I do know is that over the last five years, there has been a-knocking on my heart to do a book on Faith in the Real Estate industry. It knocked loudly in January of 2017, and I pushed it down, redirecting my focus to other things. But while laying in bed February of 2019, I knew that it was time. The Holy Spirit impressed on my heart that the voices of those who could help someone else needed to be heard. I no longer could wait, and be disobedient and turn a "blind eye" to the human need within real estate professionals.

As I struggle, myself, to write and reflect these words, my own feelings of loss, of failure, flood upon me. How could I lead the publication of a book when I have experienced similar emotions such loss and feelings of inadequacy and failure? That is why I am to share. Perhaps there is someone out there that will read my story, and the stories of others in this book, and be reminded that God has you. Your value is not a sum of accomplishments, or failures. Your value and success is based upon God's view of you. You are not alone. He has the final say of what you are for Him. He will take the loss and turn it into a blessing to tell His story of restoration.

The pathway to this book began in October of 2015. The year of 2015, had so many ups and downs. I had started off the year with a bang thinking that I would be partnering, *for life*, with one of the most successful real estate brands for massive global expansion. But going to the Keller Williams convention on this venture was heartbreaking.

What was to be an expansion, was the start of a crumble in many areas.

Have you ever had the start of a year kick off with possibilities and hope and within the first few months? Ever been shaken down to your core? Ever felt in your soul, "Why even have these hopeful opportunities to begin with?" Well, that was how it was in 2015.

I had worked for two decades in the real estate world: from buying my first property at 19 years old, to agent, sales trainer, to being a National Speaker for Realtor.com. My experiences took me on the path of growing the leading real estate branding, marketing and technology company for Real Estate Teams. I had the privilege of helping many get listed in the Wall Street Journal, RealTrends, and on big stages. With time, dedication, and effort, I had grown my brand to being a sought-after speaker for conferences, published a best seller in business and sales and was a successful CEO with a strong coaching practice. Yet, with all that success, my heart would tell me that there was something *MORE* out there. But going to this particular Keller Williams convention on this venture was heartbreaking. The leader never knew how I was treated at that event. I never told her.....

Within days of returning from Keller Williams convention. in 2015, my heart and soul hurt so bad I literally couldn't speak without crying. Kurt, my husband, tried to be understanding, but he had not been there. He had not gone through the pain I had experienced there. For days, following the return from the convention, there was a very dark cloud over my heart. It was no wonder that by the time October came later, it was a tipping point of wanting to move on. So much so that I said to my friend Vickie, "I want to forget real estate...I will never go to a convention, ever again... I want to forget it all..."

That day, in October, was the weekend of the Women of Faith Conference. Vickie and her sister lived in Virginia Beach, but had come to Charlotte to go to the conference. Earlier that month, Vickie had told me she and her sister had tickets to the conference, and if I wanted to join them that I could go online and get a ticket, as well as room with them. While driving down the highway, a fellow coach and speaker called me. She went on to say that she had heard that one of my closest friends had called her to tell her that she had dropped her business partnership with me. The woman had called her, firsthand, to tell her where I had taken the high road. That friend was someone like FAMILY to me for over 15 years, to the point that her business became my business. Looking back now, that was probably a catalyst for a lot of the pain in my life running my company. I worked so hard for validation and love that clients became family members, and often higher in priority than my own family.

That call, that day, brought such deep agony that when I hung up the phone, I said to Vickie, "I want to forget real estate…I never want to be in the real estate industry again or go to any convention. I am DONE!"

BUT GOD.

If you have read any of my other books, you know I say "BUT GOD," often. Isn't it so true? Even when we make our own declaration, He still stands in His calling on us. Sharing this with you, I think about the scripture of Proverbs where it says,

"Trust in the Lord with all your heart and lean not on your own understanding. In all your ways acknowledge Him and He will make your paths straight."
- Proverbs 3:5-6

This weekend of the Women of Faith Conference was no different. I bought my ticket separate from them and would be sitting in another section in the large downtown convention center in Charlotte. In the car, on the drive, I pondered to Vickie, "I wonder who I will be sitting next to at the conference."

"Whomever you are meant to be sitting by." she replied.

Pushing away the conversations I had in the car on the way

to the conference, I enjoyed this time with Vickie and her sister. I was excited to attend the two-day conference and hear the singing and speaking from women leads such as Sheila Walsh, Sandi Patti, Thelma Wells, Patsy Clairmont, and more. When we got into downtown Charlotte we checked into our hotel, changed clothes, and headed to the convention center.

Upon checking in Vickie and I went our separate ways to find our seats. I was in the VIP floor section. I found my seat on the floor level and sat down. Around me were women from all over. They announced that over 7,000 women were there together. Behind me on the second level were Vickie and her sister. I waved my arms so they would know where I was.

Here in this moment, I knew my heart was longing for the spirit of God to speak to me. I had just signed the official paperwork to sell my company to another competitor and I was ready to start a new beginning in my life in coaching and training with the John Maxwell organization, incorporating art and journaling. After all, I had declared I was done with real estate...BUT GOD!

Kicking off the convention, the music filled the room and I opened my journal to write, while feeling the spirit of the Lord. I was here to get healing; healing from all the pain of 2015. (If you want to learn more about that, read my books *Unlock Your Inner Warrior* and *Resilience In The Storm* that share this journey).

I took in everything around me and prayed for God to speak to me during this event–reveal my calling and purpose. During a break, I turned to the ladies beside me to say "Hello." When I looked at the older woman, and the younger woman next to her, they looked familiar to me. In casual conversation, I said, "Where are you ladies from?" The younger woman responded and said they were from the

Richmond, Virginia area. Looking at her, again, I couldn't shake the vibe like we had met before. So, I continued.

At this point, I was not as strong in my prophetic gifts as I would be today or perhaps I was since I had this inner knowing.

"May I ask what you do for a living?" I inquired of her.

"We are in real estate. Why do you ask? What do you do?"

"Oh, well," I stammered. "You just seem so familiar. I have taught some courses for NAR, written a real estate book, and some other things." I said generally not wanting to go into detail.

"What is your name?" she asked.

"Tricia Andreassen."

"Wait. Wait. WAIT! We are your clients!" she exclaimed.

Right there, in that moment, I began to cry. Blown over! Out of over 7,000 people around me, I had been seated by my own clients! Seated next to clients of my company I had just *SOLD*–no one knew, yet.

A couple of minutes later, the woman on stage said, "These women beside you today, and tomorrow, are your friends. We are here to support and help each other." My heart ached and I turned to them and said, "I would like your prayers. I want you to know I will be there for you and help you, but in confidence, I have just sold Pro Step Marketing. I feel like God wants to do something uniquely different in my life and I am here to listen to Him and do what He wants for me."

Just hours before, I had been in my car saying that I wanted to get away from real estate, and here God had put me next to these incredible women that were my clients. Those two women hugged me, supported me over those two days. While hearing the speaking topics and singing, I allowed the Holy Spirit to pour into me. Diverging from my past focus, I felt that I was to lead on a stage, like this, but not about marketing and business topics. Focusing on faith—heart, healing, strength, and leadership in life.

That day I had been hit by what one of my mentors would say, **'A Cosmic 2x4'** yet still I didn't fully embrace what He was trying to show me—too many emotions to still process through.

As I share this with you, I sometimes question myself how I could have done things differently, or what decisions I could have made better, if not experiencing PTSD that year and the awakening of my past childhood abuse. Understanding now that those memories were below the surface at my Keller Williams conference which clouded my judgement on how I was perceived and treated. And, at the same time, with different decisions, I might not be sharing these words, have started my publishing company, started *Unstoppable Warriors United* or have gathered these leaders for this book.

One thing I am sure of is that we must hold on, and share our joys and sorrows along the way with others so know they are not alone. That value does not come from a list of accomplishments or how hard we work, but from God. Value comes from His purpose and direction—in the highs, and the lows. We must persist in the pursuit of FAITH. I don't mean faith in the religious connotation. I mean faith as believing in what is stated in **Proverbs 3**. If we give up our faith, we give up the ability that tomorrow is a day for new beginnings, new opportunities, and new hope. We give up believing that there is a heavenly Father that loves us, and goes before us guiding our ways.

That is what I want this book to do for you. No matter what your 'religion' is, I want this book to cross borders. I want us to become a tribe; a community; a united group that can support one another through the storms and celebrate in the moments of triumph and carry one another through and beyond tough times.

Beyond this book, there is a vision. This vision is a conference where we worship and we learn...TOGETHER. We gather together to:

Pray together

Support and Encourage one another

Mentor each other

Worship together

That is my dream and vision for us. I know that God has led all of us for a purpose. What I have learned is: It is not about the occupation, or title, of what we do. It is the IDENTITY IN WHICH WE OPERATE AND SERVE. Occupation allows for connection, but God wants us to be reminded that Jesus was a carpenter, Moses was a shepherd, David was a warrior, Elisha was a farmer, and Ruth was a field gatherer–ALL were called to serve. When we are called, we are called. Standing alone in the field, working and serving, can cause our faith in something to be weakened and tested. Standing together will build our faith in Him, and in one another, to be able to carry on, to be–*unstoppable!*

How To Build Your Faith

1. Have you felt that God was speaking into your heart about something but you ignored it? Why?

_____

_____

_____

_____

_____

2. How strong is your faith right now on a scale of 1-10? What do you think, feel, know needs to happen to get to a 10?

_____

_____

_____

_____

_____

3. How much do you think your business would improve if you put your faith in God instead of other people?

_____

_____

_____

_____

_____

4. What do you need to let go of to grow your belief in yourself and in what God can do in your life?

_____

_____

_____

_____

_____

About Tricia Andreassen

Tricia Andreassen has a mission—a "life calling" she describes like this:

"My mission is to bring teaching and strategies to breakthrough challenges, struggles, and obstacles that show up daily in our business and personal lives. Each person has a purpose and calling. I want to help as many people as possible discover what God has placed in their heart to do."

As a young entrepreneur, Tricia bought her first real estate investment property at age nineteen, became a manager of a real estate company and continued on as National Speaker for Realtor.com where she trained real estate professionals how to market themselves on the Internet. Seeing a need in the real estate industry, Tricia started Pro Step Marketing and Advertising in grass roots fashion from the bonus room of her house and grew it into one of the most internationally recognizable companies within the real estate technology space. After almost fifteen years as a CEO and CMO she sold her company to expand her professional speaking, coaching practices, and training programs in the Christian faith. Her business book Interfusion Marketing hit #1 in less than five hours and remained on the best-seller list for fifty-nine weeks. She now is a multi best selling Author in the Christian Living genre addressing topics such as resilience, courage, hope, and more.

John Maxwell, the world's #1 ranked leadership expert, has certified Tricia as both Speaker and Coach to teach leadership, personal growth, and youth development programs. Her credentials also include an Executive Coach ACTP certification through the International Coaching Federation that positions Tricia to bring creative strategies to organizations, schools, ministry groups, and leaders from all walks of life. Her coaching practice is unique in bringing forth the strengths that lie within so they are maximized in business, in life and in relationships.

As her mission progresses, Tricia's growing life story continues to be told with a central message of persistence, resilience, and faith woven into insightful strategies that heal the soul and create breakthrough. Her passion is to creatively deliver, inspire, motivate, and to bring lasting change through writing, speaking, teaching, the arts (including songwriting) in intimate gatherings such as workshops and retreats that focus on unlocking inner warrior strength. While having a focus on the spiritual, Tricia brings this understanding into the company workforce environment through Organizational Development, Digital Marketing Campaigns, Sales Training, People Management, and DISC Behavioral Consulting.

To inquire about Tricia's speaking topics, private coaching or group programs email Warrior@MsUnstoppable.com.

Contact Tricia

- Website: www.UnstoppableWarrior.com
- LinkedIn: www.LinkedIn.com/in/TriciaAndreassen
- Facebook: www.Facebook.com/UnstoppableWarrior
- YouTube: www.UnstoppableWarriorWithin.net
- Twitter: www.Twitter.com/TriciaSings
- Books: www.TriciaAndreassenBooks.com
- Radio: www.UnlockYourInnerWarrior.com
- Songs: www.IgniteTheFireSongs.com
- Speaking Inquires: www.MsUnstoppable.com/Contact
- Retreats, Conferances, and Masterminds: www.WarriorGatherings.com

✝

Chapter 2

Faith and Resilience in the Storm

BY TRICIA ANDREASSEN

"Storms make trees take deeper roots."
– Dolly Parton

Have you ever watched intensely the movement of a tree when a storm is upon it? With the wind and the rain, it somehow stays rooted in its foundation underneath. Leaves may blow off some of the branches. Some of the branches may fall away and still the heart of the tree stays strong in the face of some of the most incredible seasons that could cause it to die. Yet, somehow, the tree stands. Sure, it may experience some damage. It may look like it has taken a beating. Then as the weather changes into the bright glow of the sun above, and the peace of the wind rustles through the leaves, it blossoms from that storm. The rain that came was divinely prepared to take that rainwater and nourish the heart of that tree so that it would thrive. Blossoms emerged from the combination of that rain and the rays of the sun; casting down its nutrients so it could be better than what it was from before.

That is what comes to my mind, spirit, and soul when I think of resilience. It is standing in the storm. It is having the faith and hope that you will not only rebound but you will come out stronger than before.

Perhaps that is what I was thinking the week of Christmas 2015 when I was up at my 4:30am writing time. I was at my husband's family home in Michigan. The only one up in the house, drinking my coffee with my candles lit beside me, a feeling of contemplation came over me. I was reflecting on what the last year and a half had been like. It was sincerely some of the worst times since I had experienced a miscarriage and divorce in 1997. I was thinking in this moment, "I have come through the other side…I have weathered through the worst, and I am still standing strong."

And in that moment I did feel that. I had the sense of optimism and of hope for this next chapter of my life. I had sold my company that I had worked a third of my life to build and would give me financial freedom. I had prepared…I had chosen a company that I believed was reputable based off of perceptions of others. Did I have an intuition that maybe the transaction shouldn't be trusted? Yes. But, I pushed it off my mind in hopes that my sixth sense was off. I was so ready for this new chapter of my life to do what I felt God had called me to do that I took things into my own hands on who I decided to sell to; even though my intuition was telling me something.

My evolved sense of intuition has always been strong.

Leadership expert John Maxwell commented in a teaching session one day. He said, "Prayer is when you talk to God. And intuition is when God is talking to you." That caused me to commit to memory and write that down. And yet, I have been guilty of not listening to what God may be saying at the time. I have met people in a moment and have been able to know the truth. It is in those moments he doesn't leave me. He teaches me. He guides me. He provides me resilience. Through these moments I have gained incredible insight that now has taught me to truly walk in the direction of where God is ordering my steps. I lay every relationship, opportunity and even business client on the altar, taking it to him first. If it were not for the lessons that are provided in moments of challenge I would not have that wisdom today. It is something that is so priceless I wouldn't change it for a thing.

Let's go back to that morning of when the intuition of the word 'resilience' came to me. It was the little voice inside me that said, "Tricia, you need to gather people together to share their story on the topic of resilience." The thought inspired me; hungry to learn more about how to build resilience. In my mind, I also rationalized to myself, "Just look at you, Tricia. Look at all the things you have gone through and now it's time to share your story of resilience." Little did I know that I had no idea the level of resilience I would learn in comparison to what was to come over the next six months. It would prove that resilience is not a 'one-time' thing. It is an ever-growing, ever-evolving process of growth and awareness.

I personally have come to understand that one of the key principles in holding on during a storm of adversity is having those in your life that can be there to lift you up in the right time.

I am thankful to my Heavenly Father today that I was able to stand. In reflection of telling you this story I KNOW, He brought me through.

"Therefore everyone who hears these words of mine and puts them into practice is like a wise man who built his house on the rock. The rain came down, the streams rose, and the winds blew and beat against that house; yet it did not fall, because it had its foundation on the rock. But everyone who hears these words of mine and does not put them into practice is like a foolish man who built his house on sand. The rain came down, the streams rose, and the winds blew and beat against that house, and it fell with a great crash."
- Matthew 7:24-27

After Christmas 2015 and the selling of my company, our family decided to move to Georgia. I personally felt I needed a fresh start. I didn't want to drive by my old office building anymore. I loved my parents and at the same time, the emotional responsibility was challenging at times. I had just gotten the first installment of payment for the sale of my company and was on schedule to receive six figures from the sale which would give me a foundation for my growing publishing and education company as well as my creative work, speaking, and media which I felt heavily called to do as a ministry. At this time our teenage son Jordan was facing his own challenges as many teenagers do and well, we all decided that moving would be a great new chapter. We had vacationed in Jekyll Island Georgia quite a bit over the last several years, and I had written down in my journal that we would have a place there someday. The first week of January we drove down to look at properties.

I was optimistic. I was holding on to the vision that 2015 was behind me. I made the decision that all of the pain, loss, and heartbreak I had experienced in that year was over. Opportunities presented themselves with me doing life, spiritual and leadership coaching and people continued to reach out to me about wanting help to become a published Author. I felt our family was on our way to leaving the past behind with a fresh start. We rented a house on five acres outside of Kingsland Georgia with a pond and an art/recording/author studio for my work. We listed our home for sale in North Carolina feeling confident. I was also scheduled to receive the next payment of my company sale which would be coming every four months. It gave the financial security that everything was coming together.

But just like weather conditions can change, the storm clouds began to thicken.

Anyone who has ever been in the beginning of a thunderstorm knows when a simple thunderstorm goes from being a sucker punch to an all-out tornadic event. I don't know how else to describe it but it was the cherry on top of what I felt was devastating to me emotionally in 2015. Mid-February rolled around, and the purchaser of our company defaulted on their schedule payment. My intuition had given me the sense they might not pay based on their previous months' actions, but I hoped that I was wrong. I wasn't.

When you are expecting six figures over a few months to hit your bank account, and you have to dip into savings, 401k and borrow money, you feel like you are holding on to the hope of it will work out. But the reality of the storm that was now brewing started to sink in. Our attorney advised that they were in default and had decided not to pay, so we needed to get our legal team together. For someone who doesn't like conflict and wants to believe the best in people it was very hard; very hard. I held on to the hope that they would honor their commitment. And yet when things didn't resolve, I had to stand strong.

Isn't that what resilience is? Standing strong even when every single thing is swirling around you in a storm that you can't control? So I stood.

During this time I was experiencing deep pain in my left shoulder (my dominant side). I had some cortisone shots a few months earlier, hoping it would improve but it got to the point I had to get an MRI. The result showed that I had a labral tear (cartilage) around the shoulder and that I needed surgery. I remember being on the phone with the insurance company getting clarity of what the bill would be because of the situation we were in. It had been years since I had struggled financially like this. I was being tested not only physically but spiritually and financially. After surgery I was told that I not only had a labral tear, I also had rotator cuff tear and bicep tear. It was a doozie. I would not even be able to start physical therapy for six weeks.

I made a decision to focus on what I could control. Some of my lifelong tools for resilience has been to write, paint, and sing. Prior to my shoulder pain, I was writing every day and doing creative art projects on the weekends. As my shoulder function diminished, my hand could no longer hold a pencil and the typing on the computer was too painful. I focused on pouring into myself in study and learning. I listened to audio books and focused on setting positive energy in motion every day in my attitude, actions and activities. Pastor Steven Furtick, ministered to me through his audio books every day and at all hours of the night. I felt I had found someone that was in alignment with my heart and mission. I watched the Elevation Church channel on You Tube that poured into my heart the teachings about how to focus your thoughts and the power of mindset. The heartbeat of my life work took stronger roots in the knowing I would deliver my experiences, the power of resilience and God's grace through my writing, speaking, singing and songwriting as well as helping other people share their encouragement through becoming published. I experienced God's provision first hand in the power of bringing people together to share their stories. They laughed and cried in conversations with me. They probably had no idea how much they were doing for my spirit. The beauty in this reflection today is God was at work during this storm.

The pain can come in such a force in the storm yet out of the pain a blessing beyond what you can imagine will be provided if you allow it. You must seek the lesson and the gift in all of it. Today I am so joyous, I am sharing this as I am literally on fire in my soul for my life.

For in August of 2014 while in Hilton Head on vacation, I had dropped to my knees and gave everything over to God to a level that I had never known so deep. I prayed out, "God, I can't do this anymore. I give you my work. I give you my company. I give you my family. I give you my health. I give you my pain. I give you everything. I need you to handle this now." What I know is that for him to make these changes, storms were going to be needed for the massive shift in my life. I was experiencing two parallel paths; one of amazing experiences of the spiritual gifts he was pouring into me and one of struggle and pain that I realize now was GROWTH. He was planting the seed for growth to combine with the rain of the storm so it would bring forth great things; things I just couldn't see yet.

"For I will pour water on the thirsty land, and streams on the dry ground; I will pour out my Spirit on your offspring, and my blessing on your descendants."
- Isaiah 44:3

The storm changed to an "all-out" hurricane...

Two weeks after my shoulder surgery April 2016, we had a family emergency with my son resulting him going to the hospital and being there for five days. I remember that day well and every part of me shaking. Any of us that have children know that your heart can feel like it is being ripped out during moments like this. Thank God for Vickie Smith as I talked to her on the phone while standing in the parking lot of the hospital. She held me up emotionally through my tears and stood by me. Text messages from many came through with support that I needed more than ever. People joined together in prayer for my family. This is where I continued to learn the real depth of resilience and how to PRAY like never before. I can't tell you that every day I was filled with knowing that God was watching over me. Some days it was a struggle. Sometimes I wondered if He was really listening. It was in those times that unique affirmations gave encouragement to press on and I knew God was there.

Authentic friends who have real love and believe in you = resilience.

It was a couple of weeks after this experience that my husband and I talked. We were in Georgia, but we got a message indicating our house had suffered some storm damage, and it would be at least $10,000 to do the work and go through the insurance process. I remember that night thinking to myself, "Really? How much more of this is going to continue?" It seemed every which way we went; we hit a road block. Our son missed his hometown and wanted to be back near his friends. We couldn't continue carrying two house payments for many more months. Something had to change. We made the decision to take the home off the market and move back to North Carolina. To say it was HARD would be an understatement. I had thought we were settled. I thought this was what we were supposed to do. And now, I was questioning all my decisions that I had made over those last few months. I was asking myself questions like "God, I understand I need to be here but why? What will my neighbors think?" Prior to our move to Georgia, I had experienced some of the worst betrayal and friendship loss in my life as well as past memories of sexual abuse as a child (I am grateful to say that in this deep spiritual work I have been called to do that I have been freed from those chains of burden; forgiveness, understanding and empathy for those who have gone through this is now something I can bring into my coaching and teaching.) Friends that I had for over a decade, that I thought I could count on, left.

In this season of about 16 months, we had multiple scenarios of challenge. Kurt's dad went through major surgery and almost died (but they revived him) on the operating table, my father had shoulder surgery and I was faced with choosing love and forgiveness of things that happened growing up. Our camper was broken into at a storage facility for boats and recreational vehicles. Our canoe was stolen out of our waterfront marina. My sister got injured in an attack while on school property from a student (she is a teacher) and had major surgery and extensive physical and emotional therapy.

On the business side my company was thriving and my status continued to grow due to my speaking and my book gaining international attention. However, the stress of my personal hurting within my heart gave rise to physical illness and making my intuition and decision making weaker than normal. Luckily, I had my Director of Operations, Dara, who oversaw the projects and ran implementation. All ran smoothly on that end. The sales side was another story as in these moments to build revenue, I had trusted someone as a strategic partner to offer additional services to our clients. I opened my heart, my home environment, and my office to this person. During this time they wanted to buy my company of 14 years which was well established. The offer however, was they wanted to purchase the company in offering stock for their existing company. Thank goodness my husband was in those meetings and began to ask questions and research public records in regards to their company. It was uncovered that about 50% of their existing clients were one's we had helped them acquire. Their stock was worth less than a penny and after much logical thought we denied their offer to purchase us. In that decision they gained access to my company client list (database) and was prospecting our customers behind our back. It was in the middle of this that my intuition came back into focus. I am certain God placed on my heart and in my husband's mind the awareness. Both of us had been thinking (and had not shared with each other yet) that something seemed off and we should do a Google search into this person's name. Over many days of research and the hiring of a private investigator we uncovered that this person had created an alias name and had a Federal criminal record for SEC fraud; banned for life from stock trading. It was compounded even more when we tried to share this with a friend of 14 years (I thought a best friend as we talked almost every day). I had gone to her birthday events, traveled on trips with her and gave not only my heart but my business expertise to help her in all ways. It was a blow when we got a cease and desist showing her exact words that I had told her to research on her own before making any big decisions (I didn't want to disclose anything else as I was mindful of legalities). It was in that experience I couldn't even warn my clients because of the threats I was receiving. I am not exaggerating when I tell you that I feared for my safety and my families' safety after what was discovered through the investigations and court documents. That was the ultimate breaking point for me emotionally as my heart was broken so severely; into what I felt was a million little pieces. And in December of 2015 the relationship with my friend was confirmed when she said to me that our friendship had been more business than personal. I felt that I had been used all those years for my free business insight where I normally charged for it.

When we moved back into our home in North Carolina I got a knock on the door from the local sheriff. I was notified several thousand dollars' worth of jewelry was stolen by one of the movers and they had retrieved some items during another investigation in a neighboring town. The only way this was brought to my attention was my recovered high school class my full name engraved on it and the police was able to locate me easily on the search engines due to my experience in business.

During this season of storms, my resilience was strengthened. When things happened in 2015 I have to admit it, some of those days I found it difficult to even get out of bed much less talk to anyone in that season. My heart was sincerely broken and my faith had been shaken deeply. I felt alone in my faith. So, when I moved back to North Carolina where there was so much pain associated with it, this was a test of my resilience. I am so very thankful for my husband as he was and is always my strength, best friend, and provider. The gift in this storm was he began to seek God's words and prayed with me. We realized we had to go with the flow like the highs and lows of the tide. I am grateful that God was right there with me through it all. During the end of 2014 and in 2015, the friends and people that were poisonous in my life were being cleared away for me to move into God's calling on my life that I had known so many years ago. Some of these relationships were what I now recognize as co-dependent. I remember being told by my great friend Coni Meyers that our greatest strength can also be the greatest weakness. Because of my heart and having such a strong desire to be there for people (that was where I found worthiness, significance and contribution) I have been blessed to have my emails full of messages thanking me for prayers and other things to help them through.

On the flip side, it has caused great persecution in that some do not understand my heart and the calling on my life for the work God has called me to do. Even in the most recent season I was told that when I was requesting prayer on social media for a friend or raising donations for clothes for a family in need that it was to just gain attention. The hard part of these comments came from those I thought were leaders in Christ. Instead of talking on the phone with me about my "WHY" and wanting to gain understanding, they chose texting on social media to use words that were negative. The enemy tried over and over again to thwart me from standing in the gap for those in need and showing what living a Christ inspired life is all about. That is why I have a group on Facebook specifically dedicated to this as all of this has brought greater understanding to the scripture that Apostle Paul wrote in 2 Corinthians 12:10, "That is why, for Christ's sake, I delight in weaknesses, in insults, in hardships, in persecutions, in difficulties. For when I am weak, then I am strong."

The church I had been attending prior to Elevation Church had not felt like a fit. The day after I gave my only signed copy of "The 21 Laws Of Leadership" and a gift of funds to buy the pastor John Maxwell's Leadership Bible, I knew in my spirit that the "Law of the Lid" applied in this case. My earned maturity (yes that is what resilience brings!) showed that I needed to find a church where the leader had a vision as monumental as me. As my strength in my knowing of who I was meant to be for the rest of my life my sweet friend Tracy of 15+ years invited me to Elevation Church.

She had also been in a difficult season of divorce after 25 years and was working on growing her walk with God. That was another deep layer within the threads of resilient strength; strength and a mission that has grown into an unstoppable movement. Isn't it incredible that we can look back at the storm we have come from and realize what we learn from it? It is in this knowing that I am more trusting in the process because God has always carried me through. The gift in this has been the understanding of what Jesus and the disciples went through carrying the word of God throughout the land and often being criticized by those who were supposed to be of like mind and faith. It is in the knowing that others do not have your calling. They do not have your vision. They do not see what God sees in you. They do not understand what God is doing THROUGH you! As you see, there have been unforeseen gifts that have come to the surface in this journey. The Holy Spirit continues to strengthen my gifts that have allowed me to work intimately with those who are experiencing loss, transition, and pain in their soul; fighting to find their way back to who they were called to be.

"Very truly I tell you, whoever believes in me will do the works I have been doing, and they will do even greater things than these, because I am going to the Father. And I will do whatever you ask in my name, so that the Father may be glorified in the Son. You may ask me for anything in my name, and I will do it."
– John 14:14

When the celebration and successes come, you also must know that is when the enemy will attack you. This can make you lose momentum or just simply quit.

I remember the first few days coming back to North Carolina, after being in Georgia those short few months and questioning all of the last year. Even though I had been strong, I had a moment of inadequacy. I was wondering if I was enough; good enough; and was failing. One day while on the phone with Co-Author Mark Williams I was in the parking lot of my physical therapist after the session. I was crying. It was my first few days back to North Carolina and I felt lost. I shared with my friend what my mind was telling myself, "Am I not moving forward now that I have moved back to North Carolina?" All the memories of the business and personal loss were a stronger reminder here in the town where I had experienced so much. In a powerful moment he said to me something I will always remember. "Tricia," he said. "God wants you to know that you have come back as a conqueror. The reason you are back is he has more for you to do here that you don't see yet." As I went to my church, sang, studied and worshiped I knew he was right.

With friends in my life, the resilience skills, and staying focused on God's grace of seeing me through, I often ask myself how is it that I have come through difficult chapters with such a certainty; a knowing that I will make it through? I know, and yet the word I am going to use is one that is a mystery.

It is FAITH.

Many hear the word faith and religion comes to mind. But what comes to me is having the perseverance to not give up no matter what and know that you will somehow, someway come out through the other side. Now does this mean I don't experience doubt? Of course not. Doubt is not the opposite of faith, and neither is fear.

Faith is holding on to the root and believing that even if you can't see the green above the soil that it is somehow working to create something better.

Over the years of my life, I have learned that I can't make assumptions on what should happen. Only God can direct my path. And with him, I can direct my actions, my mindset, and my attitude. Speaking of mindset however; faith is not a mindset either. We may think it is on the surface when we catch ourselves saying, "I have faith." What I have found that mindset does not make up the entire landscape. Without the daily action of moving forward in some way things would never have an opportunity to evolve. I think back to when I was just 19 years old. I had been working my way through college and was given the opportunity to work for a local real estate company. In that experience, I met some wonderful mentors who saw something in me and took the time to see the drive within my heart to succeed in life. I ended up buying my first investment property on my own. I was so very proud of myself to do this without even my parents knowing. I studied the classes of Dave Deldotto and Robert G. Allen. I sat at the housing office on campus at Virginia Tech and did my own interviews with potential tenants. I matched people together and filled up the rental property. I was mentored by a local real estate attorney and he had me manage his properties for him. I was so excited at the opportunity to grow in business. Being raised in a trailer most of my life except for just a couple of years, I had an intense desire to live somewhere that I could be proud of.

Then things changed. I met a young man and fell in love with him. Again, from just weeks after the start of dating, I didn't listen to the intuition that this person could be verbally abusive and have other issues. All I saw was the possibility in the future of being with someone who was getting his Engineering degree and had a strong desire for money. My craving for wanting to be loved blocked the senses of trouble that his family had experienced financial problems and possible bankruptcy. With my blinders on, I didn't think anything of it when he wanted to purchase the other rental properties with me. So, I moved forward in the process. As things in the relationship became more abusive evolving into an eating disorder and unworthiness so came the financial side of the fall as well. I won't go into the details of all of it here, but I can tell you when you walk into your home and find that everything was taken from it: the light fixtures on the walls, the washer and dryer and even the promise ring that was given (but paid for on my credit card), it can knock out almost any chance of a comeback. Thankfully, what I was able to muster in me was a faith that somehow I would find a way back to myself. If I had not had faith, I would have quit right there, but I found a way to push through the feelings of failure in my real estate ventures and get my real estate license. By the time I was 23, I was managing a real estate company office and by the time I was 27, I became the first woman National Speaker and Trainer for Realtor.com. That led to training REALTORS® on marketing and sales, being a national continuing education instructor and eventually the sales trainer for the national sales force of Realtor.com.

So as I reflect on this chapter in my life, I could not have had resilience without faith. In the book of Hebrews in the Bible it says "Faith is the substance of all things hoped for, the evidence of things not seen." - Hebrews 11:1. Oh how that rang true and it is a fundamental foundation in my life. I hoped for something more. I had NO EVIDENCE of what could be at the time. My credit was ruined. I felt ugly at 5'8 and 120 pounds yet my mom was worried at my anorexia (and she had no idea of my eating disorder and the fine line of bulimia sneaking into my life). I felt like I was a failure at love. I thought I could never go into real estate since I had lost my property to foreclosure. Yet...somehow I believed in myself; a place deep down inside me. I kept moving forward. Some days were easier than others, but I made a decision to refuse to quit but only because I held on to the provision that things would align and work out. I remember one night driving the car and thinking logically, "If I just took my car over this mountain, all of this would go away. I would die and just not be a burden anymore and I wouldn't have to face all this pain." Thank goodness I know God was right there with me, and he put the strength in me to persevere.

I am grateful for that as I experienced a divorce and miscarriage all within one year at the age of 26. If I had not had faith in myself, I would have not had the courage to move my life back to Virginia with little money in my pocket (and leaving my established real estate practice). I would not have seen the job posting for that National Speaker position for the internet site for the National Association of REALTORS®. I would not have had the persistence to call headquarters and ask them if they wanted to meet me in person (even though I was in VA with little resources and was offering to fly to California for the interview!). I didn't see the entire outcome of the situation at that moment. All I did was take a step of actions. After the first interview that day in California, I was offered the job. About a month later my boss and I were traveling to Palm Desert to speak to the REALTOR® Association and she said to me, "You know why I hired you, right?" I just looked at her not exactly knowing how to respond. "When I was interviewing you I saw an angel standing beside you." I thought she was crazy at that time but after my intensive angelic experience in the beginning of 2015, I know that God was revealing the higher calling, the next step of work I was to do. In writing this, I have to say THANK YOU to my Heavenly Father right now for being there for me in the darkest of storms in my life.

Faith = the cornerstone of resilience.

No wonder in the Bible there is the scripture in James 2:14, "Faith without works is dead." We can't sit around saying I have Faith and think it will work. We MUST to some type of work to put into action so the faith shows up. It is what I have learned to do over the trials in my life. I remember talking with a friend about the chapters in my life and she said, "Tricia, you should write a book about how to start over because you have been so good at it with such focus and an optimistic view."

How did I get good at it? I have put into practice ways to build my resilience in the storm. I have come to realize that without the storms there would be no rain. Without the rain, there would be no flowers. Without the flowers there would be no beautiful blooms; the blooms of opportunities; of miracles.

The gift of resilience.

The tools I had put into practice and have learned, has created the path for me to move forward more efficiently. Within days of moving back to North Carolina, doors began to open. I was now able to go back to my church with pastor, Steven Furtick, with a deeper understanding of his heart and work. I don't know the how I am to work with him in his ministry and yet I have faith because I know the WHY behind it. I feel it in every part of my being. My speaking to thousands on business, leadership, and marketing will now be on a deeper level of ministry that I was called to do when I was seven years old and again at thirteen. In the going through the storms, I am much more aware of how powerful the experience is in working with others who feel broken in their spirit. I have a deeper understanding of God's timing instead of mine. All of the combinations of experience, key relationships of other thought leaders, my speaking, writing, spiritual healing work and retreats ministry continue to present what God wants for my purpose.

My publishing company and learning institute have continued to bloom out of these storms in life. I now receive the storms for I know what transformation, focus and problem solving they can bring! I get continual messages from people globally about how they have stronger faith in what they are facing. I also receive messages from CEO's that they are now sharing the vulnerability of their life journey which brings connection and authenticity to their relationships. They are building their resilience. They are inspired to keep moving forward.

If I hadn't opened the door of allowing God to work through me, these opportunities would not be here today. The vision of my life work would not be as clear as it is now.

My faith is stronger than it has ever been because I know what can be done in the midst of adversity and struggle. It is in the perseverance and the resilience in the storm that has created a blossoming of life moments for me. My family is committed to caring for one another, learning to take God's direction and truly understand what is important. Just the other day my son took my hand after church and held it. For my teenage boy to do that when most times he wants to be all grown up, my heart swelled with joy.

I find myself stronger when the storms hit, even more today than twenty years ago. You see, it grows – just like a tree in the soil. It is in those challenges that I can stand in the truth that God has me in his arms. My friends are there to pray with me and support me. My clients are there to remind me that my work is a ministry and will touch many lives for generations to come. My family is there to reaffirm what is important in this life and what needs to be most treasured. My faith and my spiritual gifts of the prophetic word give me pause to always let God lead my life instead of the other way around.

Storms always prepare us in some way for the growth that we need; even if we don't see it at the time.

Just like the tree growing in the soil, when it doesn't rain the leaves begin to wilt on the branch. When we understand that the gentle rains and the storms all contribute, it shows that it is the cycle of life and the strength of resilience.

"You heavens above, rain down my righteousness; let the clouds shower it down. Let the earth open wide, let salvation spring up, let righteousness flourish with it; I, the LORD, have created it."
- Isaiah 45:8

How To Build Your Faith

1. **Practice Mindfulness** - Have awareness your thoughts. Ask yourself questions that empower you.

What is the truth in front of me right now? (Ex: The truth is I have my family with me at this moment and God is here for me.)

_____

_____

_____

_____

_____

What can I really control? (Ex: I can control my attitude, my focus, my actions, and my mindset.)

_____

_____

_____

_____

_____

What do I need to release that I have no control over? (Ex: Other's perception of me, making them happy, etc.)

_____

_____

_____

_____

_____

What is one thing I can do to keep me moving forward; even if it just a small, baby step. (Ex: I will go for a walk and listen to a Steven Furtick message or my Audio book by Steven on Crash The Chatter Box, Elevation Worship Music, etc.)

_____

_____

_____

_____

_____

2. **Meditate and Journal** - Quiet your mind and meditate on the voice that needs to be heard. God may be trying to tell you something but you are so absorbed in the noise you can't hear it. Write your thoughts. Get them out of your head and released onto paper. It doesn't need to be perfect or seen by anyone else. Use it to work through what you need to work through in the moment.

Example writing prompts:

I am finding it hard today to feel grateful but if I had to choose just three things they would be _____, _____, and _____.

I can choose these three things because they make me realize that

_____.

I feel really frustrated about _____

but I know that feeling this way will help me _____.

3. **Have a creative and physical outlet** - You don't have to be an artist to release creative energy. It could come in cooking a meal, or even coloring in a coloring book. Go outside to get fresh air. Take a moment to look up at the sky. This may allow you to gain a fresh perspective.

What are some hobbies where you lose yourself in time and enjoy yourself?

_____

_____

_____

_____

_____

When is the last time you did that?

_____

_____

_____

_____

_____

How could you incorporate this into your life?

_____

_____

_____

_____

_____

What could this do for you personally if you incorporated this more into your life?

_____

_____

_____

_____

_____

4. Surround yourself with an inner circle that lifts you up - People that stand by you and are there to LISTEN not necessarily give advice! Those who have faith in what can be accomplished and can lift you up when you need it most. Be careful of the relationships that drain you. You know who they are.

Who do you recognize in your inner circle that helps you through challenging times and provides you positive support?

_____

_____

_____

_____

_____

Who are those in your inner circle that you need to be mindful of because of the negative energy or their lack of believing in you may bring to the situation? Why?

_____

_____

_____

_____

_____

What could you do to improve your inner circle? (Ex: I know that going to my church Elevation, helped me along with my mentorship with John Maxwell and others that had like-minded vision.)

_____

_____

_____

_____

_____

How could that build your resilience when challenges come your way?

_____

_____

_____

_____

_____

5. **Vision and/or Focus** - Keep yourself on the big picture so that you hold on hope and a promise of a better tomorrow. Example: My vision of wanting to touch the hearts and lives of others has made me not give up regardless of how bleak the moment looked.

What is your big picture? What do you want to contribute to others?

_____

_____

_____

_____

_____

To get you through a difficult moment you can make the choice to where to focus. Just like a camera that offers different sets of lens to take that picture, you can control where your focus goes and determine if it is serving you to get you through the situation.

What are you focused on? Is this view helping you to breakthrough to the other side or is it debilitating you physically, spiritually or emotionally. What could you focus on to make things better?

_____

_____

_____

_____

_____

"Energy flows where attention goes."

6. **Forgiveness** - I had to forgive. Not just others but myself. The only way to move forward is to forgive. If you don't, it can eat you from the inside out. Ask yourself these hard questions as they will be a gateway for your breakthrough.

Who do I need to forgive in my life so that my heart and mind is free to accept new opportunities?

_____

_____

_____

_____

_____

What do I need to forgive myself for? Why?

_____

_____

_____

_____

If your best friend said this to you, what would you say to them to help them release and move forward?

_____

_____

_____

_____

7. **Love** - Practice self-care and surround yourself in feelings of love. One of my greatest joys has been my two dogs, Collie-mix Riley, and my Golden Retriever Gabriella. Their unconditional love always gives me comfort. My other comfort of love is in the knowing that God is there for me. All I have to do is reach out to my Bible and read those words to be reminded of his promise. Write down your

43

insights below as this will deepen the roots of when you need to call upon resilience.

What are some situations where you felt love and connection?

_____

_____

_____

_____

_____

How could you bring more healthy love into your life?

_____

_____

_____

_____

_____

What would be some ways to love yourself more unconditionally?

_____

_____

_____

_____

_____

Journal this affirmation - If I put this into practice it would make me feel...

_____

_____

_____

_____

_____

8. **Gratitude** - Find something; anything in the moment to be grateful for. Seriously it could be as simple as "I am grateful I have coffee in my pantry. I am grateful I have socks to wear." Search for gratitude, grab it and hold on tight.

In listing my 3 things that I am grateful for I realize that...

_____

_____

_____

_____

_____

9. **Positive words** - I use positive words that I could use in the moment for moving me forward.

"God is giving me curriculum."

"The gift in this situation is..."

What could be something that you could say to yourself to reaffirm your inner strength?

_____

_____

_____

_____

_____

✝

Chapter 3

Reflecting on Your God-Given Talents and Gifts– That's Success

BY DIRK ZELLER

I must admit that my interest in real estate and real estate sales was formed in my teenage years. There was something magical about real estate properties and the people that sold and leased them. Maybe it was my first-hand experience with my parents owning both residential and commercial rentals. Or it could have been the work those properties provided for me in mowing lawns, landscaping, repairs, and learning renovation skills in junior high, high school, and college. It was what I perceived to be a pathway to wealth and financial security. I was observant of the commercial real estate brokers in their expensive suits and luxury cars, and the vibe of success and wealth that surrounded them. I knew right then, I would either invest in or sell real estate.

However, it took me until I was 28, to make my way into the world of real estate. And now, years later, I feel blessed beyond measure to have invested almost three decades of my life immersed in selling, buying, investing, renovating, and authoring books about real estate topics. I have traveled the world speaking at real estate and sales conferences, and developing and delivering programs to help agents and brokerages expand their earnings and life through real estate. I have truly been blessed by my pursuit of real estate as a career and investment vehicle. Through this journey, I have made countless mistakes and miscues. There have been epic failures; along with untold blessings.

Real estate sales is the ultimate in entrepreneurial businesses. It does not require a master's degree, nor even a college degree. The initial capital investment is low. The opportunity to earn a six-figure income and beyond is attainable to everyone. In my first full year in real estate, 1991, I earned $103,000 in gross commission. I closed 33 sales that first year in the business, so my average commission check was paltry by today's standards. Yet, that set the foundational belief inside me that I could make any amount of money that I desired. My goal in that first year was to make $100,000, and I did it with $3,000 to spare. There is no better career and business opportunity than one where the income is as unlimited as the opportunity. Real estate sales create that avenue.

When I was newly licensed, I received one of the best pieces of advice in my life. It came from my father, who was just retiring from a 30-year career as a dentist. He said to me, "Dirk, dentistry didn't create wealth for me. The real estate I invested in created the wealth. The dentistry provided the income that allowed me to save and invest in real estate." My father, because he built a solid dental practice, could secure bank financing easily to leverage and invest in real estate.

When I realized the wisdom in his statement, I decided to use his formula to invest in real estate. I went about building my real estate sales business to grow my income to a level that any bank would be happy to lend me money to acquire rental properties. This provided me income to be able to invest in real estate. My counsel to others is to use my father's same advice to recognize you will achieve wealth through owning real estate. Selling it will provide the cash flow; owning will provide the wealth. How you use your cash flow will make a difference.

Resolve to only use the net operating income to buy more investment property or pay down debt on real estate loans. Don't use the net operating income for any other purpose until you have acquired the asset base, number of properties, or number of units to achieve financial independence for yourself and your family. Resist the temptation to buy things like a new home, car, or boat with your net operating income.

Following these simple steps, advice, and wisdom have enabled me to acquire more than 70 rentals in the last ten years, alone! If I have been able to purchase enough rentals to create enough passive income to last my lifetime and beyond, it means that anyone can do exactly what I have done.

We are all blessed with unique talents and abilities for success. We also have access to formulas that others have used to achieve success. If someone has done it, that means any of us can achieve the same. I have been a conscious student of success for more than 30 years. Before that time, I was not conscious, deliberate, or focused on the pursuit of success. Up until my late 20's, I was more in the lottery category of success. What I mean by lottery is,–wishing, hoping, and gladly accepting success if it showed up on my doorstep one day.

My belief is that God desires us to achieve success. He is there to guide and protect us on our journey to success. He is a God of success. He is also there to provide comfort, healing, and learning in our failures. Some of the truest teaching moments of life come through the lens of failure.

Utmost, God's design is for our success and achievement. That doesn't mean that I believe that all of us are to be driving luxury cars, thin, and wealthy. It might not be the classic "United States version" of success, or the "prosperity gospel" version of success. Our objective should be to seek God's definition of success for us, and our lives. It is key to check, evaluate, and pray that we keep aligned with what God's definition of success is for us.

The pursuit of success is not new. People of all ages have been trying to unlock the mysteries of human behavior, peak performance, and success. Why is it that some people seem to, at first observation, achieve success easily while others try, but repeatedly fall short? Both have the desire to improve their lives, but only some of them actually achieve it.

Aristotle, who studied and wrote about success until 322 BC, said, "We are what we repeatedly do. Excellence therefore is not an act, but a habit." He was using success interchangeably with excellence. The big picture in this quote is the connection between repeatedly doing something, and the establishment of a habit. His relevant conclusion was that you can create the habit of success, or you can create the habit of failure.

Success, or excellence, can always be created through establishing positive, repetitive habits. Unfortunately, almost anything we do repeatedly can lose its luster, passion, and energy over time. Yet, without doing something repeatedly, you won't establish it as a habit. While you focus on repeating the actions that lead to success, you create successful habits. So, repeating and success are like "peas and carrots"–they go together. There is always "a yin and a yang" in the pursuit of success. Not engaging in the right actions repeatedly over time, creating bad habits that guarantee failure–yang. Right actions repeatedly done, create habits and guarantees success–yin.

We all will create habits in either direction in life. The establishment of our habits is inevitable. We are the ultimate arbiter of what those habits will be for us. First, we will create our habits, and then our habits create us.

Success is many things to different people. We all have our own personal and unique definition of what success is to us. The dictionary defines success as the fact of getting or achieving wealth, respect, or fame. It also defines success as the correct or desired result of an attempt. I feel those two definitions capture the essence and objectives of success. Too many of us attach the moniker of "Success" to the end result of achieving success: the achievement of the purchase of a new Mercedes, the finish line of becoming a millionaire, our kids graduating high school or college, or the corner office in the company. Success is not a destination, but a journey to be traveled with milestones along the way.

Earl Nightingale, still in my view, has the best definition of success. "Success is the progressive realization of a worthy goal or ideal." Earl expressed that in 1957, in his recording of *The Strangest Secret*. His recording sold more than a million copies and went viral before viral existed. The pursuit of success requires personal development, personal discipline, success habits, and understanding and utilizing your unique talents.

The biggest "isn't" of success is failing to define it for yourself, as a couple, or as a family. It's easy to get sidetracked or pursue someone else's definition of success. Our brains are bombarded with images of success in social media, news, television, or even in the parent drop-off lane at school. We can't avoid seeing Sally's new Porsche or her daughter's new designer clothes. Or we notice that Amy looks so tan and rested after her family's trip to Barbados.

Rather, observe others to encourage and remind yourself of what is possible. Don't observe to compare, or keep score. That is hard to do, especially in a business of competition like real estate sales. The truth is, the only score card that matters is yours. Being successful is granting grace to yourself and others when the achievement you desire takes a little while longer than you expected. I had a coaching call recently with a wonderful client, Sandy. Sandy's goal was to sell enough homes to make $250,000. She had a challenging year because she and her business partner decided to end the partnership halfway through the year. There was a lot of drama to say the least. We were reviewing what she had earned and what was still to be collected in income, and we came to the realization she would not make her $250,000 goal. When that fact was confirmed, she didn't feel very successful. Frequently, our timeline for success can be slightly off. In reviewing her sales numbers, I ventured that her sales in escrow that were set to close by the middle of January would put her at that $250,000 mark. So, she missed her goal, but she only missed it by two weeks. In the overall scheme of things, that's a small miss.

One of the best parts of being in real estate sales, brokerage, or even real estate investment is, there isn't only one way to achieve success. There isn't one way to generate leads in real estate, or one way to build your business. The variety of lead generation options are endless. Anytime you hear someone proclaim, "This is the only way!" to do business, you should run the other direction–fast. The vast options on "how to" create leads and business, makes real estate sales exciting and ever-changing.

While referrals should be the cornerstone and are the most important source used to generate your business, they should not be your only source. The objective should not be to be a 100% referral-based business as some "experts" express. If one studies the National Association of Realtors Profile of Home Buyers and Sellers report that is released annually, reviewing the charts, graphs, and research NAR has done on home buyers and sellers, you might be shocked that 31% of all buyers found the agent they worked with to buy a home through their online search.

What that means is, that for the 5.4 million buyers in the United States, fully 1.67 million found their agent not through a referral, but through shopping online. Can you afford to ignore 31% of all buyer prospects? How many sales per year are in your market? Pull that number up in your multiple listing service and multiply that by 31%. That's how many you have no chance of getting if your focus is 100% referral-based. Let me restate: referrals are the most important part of your business, it's just not the *only* part of your business. It's easy to lose sight of the big picture in pursuit of success. We have so many experts, new technology, change, and disruption hitting us in real estate sales. Frequently, it is better to focus and remove yourself from the noise.

I spent my whole career with one company. I didn't feel the need to change and also knew the grass wasn't greener elsewhere. In today's disrupted real estate market, that is rare. That does not mean all things were rosy with my broker, at all times. There was a time when my broker and I were going through a rough spot in our business relationship. During that rough spot, I contacted another successful broker with multiple offices who was rumored to be opening an office in my service area. We met for lunch to discuss the potential of my changing companies. After we dispensed with the initial warm-up, the first question he asked me was, "When are you going to stop all this prospecting and become a 'real' real estate agent?" I was stunned by his comment. It showed how opinionated he was about "the way to do business." We talked real estate for another 45 minutes, but my desire to go to work for him ended the instant he revealed his myopic viewpoint. I sold more houses than probably any other agent he had in his firm at that time. His view was that a "real" agent didn't prospect—especially expireds, which I did constantly and very successfully. I enjoyed the challenge of convincing a seller my approach and strategy was better. I was wired for competition with others. It's how God made me as a human being. This broker didn't understand that. He lost the chance to land a very successful agent because of his limited viewpoint.

The pursuit of success in life is the pursuit of uncovering and utilizing your talents. We all have hidden talents that were woven into you before birth. Some of those talents will surprise and delight you. Psalms 139:13 says, "For you created my inmost being; you knit me together in my mother's womb." It's clear that we each have been designed for greatness. That God has placed special talents, skills, and attributes in each of us.

> *"In his grace, God has given us different gifts for doing certain things well."*
> *- Romans 12:6*

Our mandate is to passionately pursue revealing and refining the gifts for their full use. Let me share an example based on me.

I honestly never imagined in my wildest dreams that I would ever write a book, let alone eleven of them thus far. My most recently completed was the most meaningful to me, yet. Being asked to write *Success Habit for Dummies* was a highlight in my life. It's because it replaced Zig Ziglar's *Success for Dummies*, and Zig was such a good personal friend and mentor of mine.

Additionally, when you graduate high school class that makes the top half possible–your expectations in English composition are very low. Truth be told, my mother was an English teacher. I hated English composition and I have the penmanship of a baboon. I was in my mid-thirties writing a few articles to publish in sale trade magazines and websites. I knew that my sentence structure was woefully inadequate. So, I asked my mom to edit them before I submitted them. She said she would be happy to help. So, I faxed them over to her.

I waited a week and called her and said, "Hey mom, do you have those done? I have a deadline." She said, "Yes, I got them done days ago." "Great, can you fax them back?" She said, "No, you have to come over and pick them up." Now, I knew there was more to this than just a drive across town. I thought it was a mother creating a way to require her son to stop by and see her. A few days later I stopped at my parents to pick them up. My mother proceeded to pull out the articles. I scarcely recognized them because of the red ink splashed like splatters of blood all over the pages. It was clearly a scene out of *Texas Chainsaw Massacre* on the pages of articles. She proceeded to instruct me on the basic and finer points of English composition. That moment is unduly etched in my brain even more than twenty years later. I had no idea that God placed the skill to write inside of me, but it's clearly there–with my mother's added touches.

God has placed within us abundant talents. I think His focus in not the overall number, but talents in depth, specificity, and specialty. Talents that can be developed into world-class level, world-changing talent. Some of you might be thinking that thought to be scarcity thinking. That we have countless talents. I would contend that talents that are world-class are few in each of us. My experience is that focus proceeds results or success. That we are incapable of focusing on everything or being good at everything. That we have talents and gifts in many areas but there are a few that bring us joy and impact our world significantly. Those few talents at the world-class level are why we are here.

"Success is the process of self-discovery mixed with self-discipline applied to the talents that God has given us."
- Dirk Zeller

How To Build Your Faith

1. What talents are inside of you that you haven't allowed to develop?

_____

_____

_____

_____

_____

2. What talents are inside of you that you haven't discovered?

_____

_____

_____

3. What has God put in there that you know is there, but you have underutilized it?

_____

_____

_____

_____

_____

4. What self-discipline is required to unlock the talent?

_____

_____

_____

_____

_____

Reflecting on your talents and gifts that enable you to serve your real estate clients at a world-class level is success.

The real estate industry has changed significantly in the last thirty years, and especially in the last five years. The industry has gotten more complex, fractured, technology-based and impersonal. How we go about our daily business of generating clients and serving those clients has evolved to be complex; but has it really?

Creating successful, impactful, significant service to others isn't actually contained in the complex. We might believe that, or companies who are trying to sell us something as business owners might project that, but it's false. That's a false narrative that produces distraction and overwhelm in our mind and actions.

I will admit that it's human nature to complicate things, whether that comes from a need to feel important or just human nature. I don't know exactly, but I do know that simple truths and simple formulas are the pathway to success. In real estate sales it is applying straightforward rules and formulas to achieve success and wealth. In the last six months I have been getting my coaching clients to hyper-focus on setting a specific number of appointments each week. That's a pretty simple concept and uncomplicated goal. Let's say the goal is three face-to-face appointments a week. These can't be showing appointments with buyers you have already converted to a client. They must be new prospects, past clients, or current clients provided you are asking for referrals. It's a sales appointment to create new prospects.

Here is the system: you invest Monday through Wednesday on prospecting and lead follow up to secure new prospect appointments. Let's say you manage to secure one appointment for later in the week with a new buyer. You are still two short of goal Wednesday evening. You then on Thursday and Friday start to call past clients and your sphere to secure face-to-face coffee appointments, so you can finish the week at three. If you repeated that simple process weekly, you would book 150 appointments a year. It would be almost impossible not to do 30 sales in the next 12-months from just doing this simple process.

33% of appointments would be with prospective buyers or sellers. In 50 appointments, you secure that prospect to a client 50% of the time, which is 25 clients. That's a very conservative ratio; you might be at 75%. Then 80% of those clients list or buy with you. That equates to 20 closed deals in a year.

66% of appointments would be with past clients or your sphere in a coffee meeting. You average a referral from each coffee meeting about 50% of the time. The 100 coffee appointments turn into 50 leads from those meetings. Even if the leads convert at a 4-to-1 ratio, that's 12 closed transactions. I am using conservative ratio when applying a 4-to-1 ratio.

In total, that would be 32-closed clients from the focus and simple plan and formula of getting three face-to-face appointments a week. As Jim Rohn used to say, "What is easy to do is also easy not to do." Simple formulas and simple truth are the superhighway to success.

Let me give you another way to evaluate success steps without getting overwhelmed. The power of success is contained in the Pareto Principle. The principle that 20% of your efforts will lead to 80% of the results you achieve. It's certainly a foundational philosophy of truth and success.

Diving deeper into the 20% and 80%, the truth is, the 80% of the success you experience will be achieved by executing a half-dozen things. Defining those half dozen things and focusing on consistency in doing them is being successful. The term half-dozen could be only five, or six, or even seven things. It's not more than seven. I call this whole strategy, "Disciplines of a Champion." It's what you must do consistently, then measure and monitor your results. I have included a chart and tool below to use.

1. _____
2. _____
3. _____
4. _____
5. _____
6. _____

Explanation:

What are the mandatory disciplines that will cause you to succeed regardless of economic environment or the condition of your infrastructure? Record your disciplines on the above diagram.

Examples:

- Prospect daily for two hours
- One-hour weekly coaching staff
- Two hours of planning time weekly
- Ten past client calls per day
- Monthly P&L review
- Complete coaching action plans
- One day per month reviewing your business
- 5-5-5 done daily (5 past clients, 5 new prospect calls, 5 lead follow up calls)
- One-hour lead follow-up time daily

You will notice all of these are specific, measurable, and clear. You will know instantly when you review your Disciplines of a Champion whether you accomplished them, or not.

Since the beginning of time, God designed success to be simple, not complex. He is the originator and creator of simple truths and simple formulas. The original simple formula that He shared with Adam and Eve was, "Don't eat from this tree." What did they do? They complexed it up by eating the fruit from the forbidden tree. Then God created another simple formula in the Ten

Commandments. These are the do's and don'ts and there are only ten you need to follow. What did we do with it? We complexed it up with the Levitican Laws. God then came back with the simplest truth in His son Jesus. We complexed it up through not recognizing who He was and putting him to death. The creation of simplicity is not my idea, it's God's idea. It's God's plan from the very beginning. We have to fight the urge to complex up and complicate God's divine and simple plan. Simple truths and simple formulas are God's way to achieve success.

About Dirk Zeller

Dirk started his entrepreneurial career 50+ years ago through lemonade stands. He has been creating his own economy through numerous businesses since he was 24. For more than 30 years, he has signed both the front and back of each paycheck he earned. He founded Real Estate Champions and Sales Champions in 1998. Both recognized as leading organizations in sales training and coaching in the business to consumer selling fields.

Dirk is one of the most sought after speakers in success, time management, peak performance, and sales in the world. He has presented worldwide to hundreds of thousands of entrepreneurs, salespeople, and senior executives. Dirk has been awarded the CSP, Certified Speaking Professional award from the National Speakers Association. Only 11% of speakers achieve this.

Dirk has authored more than eleven best selling books on sales, success, productivity, and time management including; *Your First Year in Real Estate*, *The Champion Real Estate Agent*, and Dummies® books; *Success as a Real Estate Agent*, *Telephone Sales*, *Successful Time Management*, and *Success Habits for Dummies*®

Dirk counts his most significant achievement to be a successful marriage of 29 years to his wife, Joan. He is blessed by his two adopted children, Wesley and Annabelle. He and his family reside in Bend, Oregon.

Contact Dirk

- Website: www.RealEstateChampions.com
- Phone: 541-383-8833

✝

Chapter 4

Let Your F-A-I-T-H Scream from the Mountain Tops

BY RICKY CAIN

Running a business can be quite challenging, and most commonly the greatest of those challenges is finding great talent to become a part of the company mission. Over a four-year stretch, our real estate company, Cain Realty Group, essentially was a revolving door. During this period, the average tenure for those we hired was just over a year. We'd spend countless hours and dollars investing in people we thought would be great fits for our company, only to part ways after several months.

This period was a tough one for my lovely bride KodiKay and I. We began to really second guess whether we actually wanted to run a business with employees, or simply work together as a two-person real estate team. We knew we cared about the people we hired. We were certain we provided more value and opportunities than most teams. So, what were we doing wrong?

Through having various business coaches and attending multiple business seminars, we learned that we needed to work on ourselves just as much as we worked on our business. We invested heavily in books, podcasts, audio books, and more. We were certain that this was the missing link between success in hiring and what we had been experiencing. While we did both grow exponentially, this didn't translate into success for our company.

We then began to think of new and exciting programs and incentives we could offer people that no one in our market was offering. Surely this would lead to us attracting top talent that could stay with the company long-term and would eventually lead to massive success within the Austin, TX real estate market. This did help us to attract a higher volume of candidates to join our team, as we were viewed as offering more than other brokerages and real estate teams.

While we were blessed to have a much larger and consistent stream of candidates, unfortunately, this didn't result in us finding like-minded individuals. Why? We were relentlessly working on ourselves. We had more to offer and more opportunities than anywhere else. Why were we continuing to have a roller coaster of a business while other large real estate teams were succeeding at a high level? What were we not doing that we should be doing?

KodiKay and I have always believed that if you are a good person at your core, if you act in others' best interests, and if you are a hard worker, then you likely would be a great fit for our company. Those were literally the things we looked for in candidates in the early days of growing CRG. We weren't as concerned about one's background, personal interests and hobbies, religious beliefs, sexual preference, etc. so long as you met the three key criteria that I mentioned. We were both raised to look at the person more so than anything else; doing otherwise just wouldn't feel right.

Going back to my childhood, I wasn't raised around prayer, church, or anything religious for that matter. My parents were free spirits, or hippies, if you will. I believe a lot of my passion for not "judging" others on anything other than them being a good person came from them, for which I am thankful. I did spend some time in churches with various friends and family over the years, but by no means did I have any sort of strong Christian upbringing. Do good by others and you were good with me.

During this tumultuous four-year period, we had a variety of different people within our company, which I thought were great! We had those that were Atheist. We had those that believed in Scientology. We had a variety of Christian faith folks. We had a variety of folks with varying sexual preferences. KodiKay and I were none-the-different, as we both are passionate about loving all people, and not just people that do and believe what we do.

The year was 2015, and members of our real estate team and I were at an annual real estate convention. We were having breakfast together before the day was to begin, and a defining moment in my career and understanding of Faith was about to occur. As we received our meals from our waitress, a few team members and I were about to say Grace prior to receiving our meal. As we began to bow our heads down, one of our team members passionately asked, "Are you kidding me?"

As we bowed our heads in prayer, I couldn't help to notice the feeling of guilt wash over me. This teammate looked at me with shock that we actually prayed together instead of just eating our meal. This discomfort could have been cut with a butter knife. It was then I learned of the team members Atheist beliefs. While it was an awkward moment I likely will never forget, it was a moment that served as the beginning of a movement that would lead to massive change in my thinking and the way I ran our business.

A few months later, this individual wound up submitting their resignation. Essentially sharing with me they felt as if they needed to pretend to be someone they were not in our environment. When I asked to further explain, they mentioned that our environment was very "Christian-like," and it caused too much stress to feel as though they needed to conform to our environment. I was taken aback, as it's not as if we have Jesus hanging from a cross in our offices, and we don't scream out "Praise Jesus," from the top of our lungs from within the office.

Three weeks after this conversation, another one of our employees came to us with her resignation, as well. We use daily affirmations as part of our coaching. We believe in them, and we even chant one as a team every morning before we begin our day. These have no religious connotations whatsoever, and they are simply designed to empower you, give you confidence and help you to work on your internal programming. When asked why we were receiving her resignation, she shared with me that the affirmations actually go against her religion. I was shocked, yet again. Come to find out it wasn't any of the words to a particular affirmation; it was the idea that we found it useful to work on our programming that went against her particular religion.

We, of course, respectfully parted ways, and it left me thinking and wondering how we can avoid these kinds of situations in the future. We certainly don't want anyone to feel uncomfortable in our environment, or with the methods we use to coach and train people we care about. KodiKay and I both had a feeling of guilt every time a new hire didn't work out, because maybe it means there was some question we failed to ask during the hiring process. Every hire that didn't work out was on us, not the hire.

In asking other colleagues, from our office what they thought about our culture, almost all of them said something about Faith or about being strong Christians. While I see this as a compliment, it's odd for KodiKay and I to hear, as we are simply being us. Upon asking colleagues specific examples of where these patterns show up, they gave me numerous examples. What I saw as normal or routine for me, others saw differently. They heard us tell clients at the end of a call, "Have a blessed day." Or they pointed to a decoration I have that says, "Be Grateful." All of the examples that were shared, KodiKay and I just feel are normal and not by any means over the top Christian. Then, a lightbulb began to burn bright in my mind.

The next day, I sat down to look at all of our job postings online. I began to wonder how we could share more of who we are so that more like-minded individuals were attracted to our company. Do I dare share that we are a Christian-based company? What if people don't want to work for us or with us because of our beliefs? That could have the opposite effect on us wanting to grow our business. How would the public react?

I began adding the following to all of our job postings. "God, Family, then Business. Every action we take reflects these core values and in this order." If we were going to make this choice, it was going to be consistent everywhere someone could find us. Next, I began to place this on all of our online websites, recruiting platforms, and more. Once I commit to something, I'm all in and there's never any middle ground.

It wasn't long before I noticed a decline in the amount of people that were applying. At first, I thought it was coincidental, yet I had tracked our numbers for so long that I could easily see the drop off. A few more weeks went by and I began to wonder if we had made a mistake. Then something magical happened. And then it happened again, and again.

At the end of a call with a potential candidate, I asked what specifically drew her to our company. I began to think I needed to ask this just in case someone didn't catch my reference to God. I'd hate for another person to come in and see that we are strong in our Faith, and then take a quick exit. As she began to answer my question, she mentioned her main attraction was that we lead with our Faith and that we place God first in all things. I was extremely taken aback the first time it happened. Then it became somewhat of a common occurrence.

The decline of candidates remained, yet those that did apply seemed to almost be bought in to us even before they would have a sit-down interview. Was this the missing piece we had long sought after? How could I expand upon this in our process?

Now that we were attracting those that had Faith just as we did, things started changing around the office. People that had Faith, yet perhaps it wasn't where they wanted it to be, started going to church more regularly. More and more people were also telling people on the phone to "Have a blessed day." This of course still makes KodiKay and I smile to this day to see people's language change. We don't ask that people on the team speak like this, they just kind of do after a few weeks within our company.

As our company continued to grow, of course there would be clients or team members experiencing tough times. Naturally, we'd want to pray for them together, as we believe in the power of prayer. KodiKay began leading these prayers, and fast forward to where we are now—it has become routine. Every morning after our coaching sessions and prior to beginning our day, someone within the company leads a prayer and everyone participates. It's quite magical, and it always sets the tone for an amazing day.

To continue ensuring we are bringing on people that want to be in this environment that's been created, we also implemented what we call a CRG Company Shadow. Since we begin each work day with prayer, I thought it would be even more important for candidates to witness this. It's one thing to say you are Christian, and it's quite another thing to pray together as a company, daily. We don't want someone realizing this on their first day working with us.

Of course, my initial thought was that we'd lose people's interest from the shadow, and quite the opposite happened. At least 70% of the time when I ask what their favorite part of the shadow was, it was that we prayed together, and we are who we portray ourselves to be online. Of course, we have the occasional candidate that finds it a bit too uncomfortable, and that's OK. KodiKay, myself, and the rest of the team take comfort in knowing those that are bought into who we are, and our environment will be happier, and that will result in us all being happier and more productive.

What I didn't expect to happen as a result of the changes we made were the deep friendships that came with it. People that were within our company suddenly became great friends, and more so, family members. In addition to our fun monthly CRG team bonding events, many of us go to church together, we play sports together and we genuinely enjoy spending time together outside of the office. In the past, we attempted to have some friendships with those we worked with at CRG, and it wound up being to our detriment. We had begun to think we couldn't have great personal relationships with people that work for our company. KodiKay and I honestly had started to build a wall around ourselves until this breakthrough happened. Now, we all are extremely close and honestly view ourselves as one big family, instead of viewing each other simply as co-workers, bosses or employees.

In an attempt for all of us to be better equipped with how to define our culture at CRG, we came up with five core values. The exercise we did as a company to choose these five core values was very insightful. We broke up into two groups and each group took an identical set of cards that all had various values for people to choose from. Once each group had chosen their five values, we wrote them down on the chalkboard for all of us to see at the same time.

At the top of the two lists was Faith! This was an amazing win for us, as sometimes we look around and things can seem too good to be true. Seeing that both groups chose that as their top pick was validation that we are doing some things right. Three of the remaining four values were also matches, with only the last value being up for debate. Cain Realty Group's core values are Faith, Growth, Passion, Integrity, and Commitment.

I'd be dishonest if I told you we don't continue to have those that don't want to work for us or work with us because of our transparency regarding our Faith. In fact, we even have people cancel their home buying or selling consultations, from time to time, because of this. I have no doubt we have lost business opportunities because of our company's decision to be so transparent with what we believe.

I think back to the way things used to be like a revolving door. I think back to all of the nights KodiKay and I would literally lose sleep over people within our organization. I also think back to all the mornings I truly wasn't looking forward to coming into the office. Our willingness to be open with our Faith and be proud of it has changed everything for us. We no longer are losing people that we want to stay connected with in business. We sleep great, now. My greatest joy is coming into the office in the morning and seeing all the CRG family.

Whatever your challenge may be, consider that your Faith will always take you to the other side of that challenge. Life is like a roller coaster for you and those around you. By sharing your Faith you will not only be blessed, you will bring in light to others that may need it equally as much as you.

"Have a blessed day!"

How To Build Your Faith

1. Where in your life can you share your passion for God more publicly?

_____

_____

_____

_____

_____

2. What are some different words you can begin using in your everyday conversations to spread joy and blessings?

_____

_____

_____

_____

3. What's a challenge in your life currently that you have yet to give to God, and are you ready to release it?

_____

_____

_____

_____

_____

4. Who in your life right now could benefit from hearing how your own Faith has gotten you through tough times?

_____

_____

_____

_____

_____

5. What are your five core values that you also look for in others you befriend, or work with in business?

_____

_____

_____

_____

_____

About Ricky Cain

Ricky Cain resides in Austin, Texas, with his wife KodiKay and son Jaxon. Together, Ricky and KodiKay are owners of Cain Realty Group, which is a residential real estate company that is powered by Keller Williams Realty. As founders and owners of Cain Cares, a non-profit that assists their past clients and their family members in severe times of need, they are able to share their skills, time, and compassion.

Ricky routinely is asked to speak at large conventions, seminars and real estate breakout sessions, routinely donating any proceeds to charities he is passionate about.

Ricky and KodiKay were also blessed to have been chosen as features in the TV show, *Success in Your City*. The show chooses entrepreneurs across the country that are using their success to give back to their community.

Keller Williams Realty recognized Ricky with two of its highest honors, both locally and regionally. Locally, Ricky was awarded the *Eagle Award*, which is voted on by all of his colleagues for demonstrating the highest level of culture within the office. Regionally, he was awarded with the prestigious *Regional Cultural Ambassador Award* and got to be recognized on the big stage at Keller Williams' annual event, Family Reunion.

Ricky's passion is to help others strengthen their faith, succeed personally and professionally, and to ensure no one he cares about has to say "no" to something they deserve a "yes" to.

Contact Ricky

- Website: www.CainRealtyGroup.com
- Facebook: www.Facebook.com/Ricky.Cain
- Instagram: www.Instagram.com/Ricky.Cain
- Email: Ricky@CainRealtyGroup.com

✝

Chapter 5
It is About Relationship

BY MELISSA CARPENTER

"Continual pursue peace with everyone and the sanctification without which no one will (ever) see the Lord."
- Hebrews 12:14

How do we define ourselves as real estate agents? We are not a spectator watching from the sidelines. It is not about real estate, either. So what exactly are we then? We are leaders. We are warriors of sorts; spiritually, mentally, and physically in pursuit of helping others. No, it's not about real estate or sales, but it is about relationships. People are impacted, not impressed, by our life and our deeds. That's a huge responsibility as a believer; more of a burden that I take on, humbly. If only each of us would adhere to The Apostle Paul's advice to continually pursue peace with everyone. What an impact we could make for the Kingdom in our profession. It took years for me to piece this together. Here is my story of growth as an agent, a mother, a wife, and as a Christian ripped from prayer journals kept along my way.

My real estate journey started back when my youngest was four, she is now twenty. My career started slowly as I had three young children, and I had worked full time in sales before my daughter's birth. My career began with the infamous phone duty, open houses and talking to my friends, family, and neighbors. I hoped to make money, with flexibility. Little did I know what to expect. In my early years, I left my kids' games and family events early to get the next lead. Over time, I built a wonderful referral business and thought I had done the right thing to move upward in my career. What I didn't realize was what God had in store for me! Did I ever ask him? Did I think I had all the answers? Some time went by and I woke up one day to the event that changed everything.

It was November of 2015 when a series of events affected me in a big way. I have always had a love for helping others and routinely felt very connected to my co-workers. I woke up to a big change. One that had happened before, and not anything someone would be shocked to hear. Occasionally, we lose jobs, friends can lose jobs; it can be a significant change. This time, it seemed like one too many. Just one more change and I suddenly felt helpless. At the same time, I had another friend hurting from other matters. This all resulted in me going into a deep depression. Each day I thought it would be better, but I just couldn't shake it.

My hope is to always be the encourager, not the one bringing others down. So, I decided to stay away from the office and work from home for a little while. Prior to this happening, I had just started a Bible study at church, and it seemed to help keep both me and my emotions grounded. Often, I would cry and felt helpless for my friend. Perhaps the tipping point, I woke up and said to myself that it is, "Time to pour positive into me!" I woke up the next morning and made it my promise to start each day with something positive. I started with positive leadership-filled stories, blogs or books. Then, I continued my Bible study and listened to worship music. Each day after I added more time to each task, and this became a routine for each day. As each day passing added up, so did a month or two pass, and suddenly, I had created this amazing habit! This routine created a habit that kept me on course during down moments and within this new routine, God was transforming me.

My heart, my path, then my future in real estate changed along with this transformation. My growth in my relationship with the Lord changed. God is my rock! The place I go during hard times. He listens to me and comforts me. This deeper relationship, in turn, transformed my business. During my quiet time, my heartfelt a tug to change this real estate thing I called "my job." My passion changed as my heart changed. My daily prayer was for God to send people to me to help, to guide, to be His hands and feet. It was no longer about real estate it was about relationships. Don't misunderstand me, I had always done the best for my clients, worked hard for them, and served to the best of my ability. Now, I listened more intently to the guidance of the Holy Spirit, as well.

Now two years later, I want to share a few of my stories from the real estate world. I don't think I would have paid attention to or have witnessed where God showed up in both my life and the lives of my clients if it weren't for my own transformation and the journals I kept that recorded the events. Here are a few.

A few years back a wonderful couple had to move their parents into assisted living. It took them a little longer to get the home ready for the market, as their parents had lived in the home for over 40 years. Once we got the home on the market, the showings started flowing in and in a short time, the home had an offer. As their agent, I had to go to the assisted living home to get signatures.

As I entered the facility I watched as the workers walked me to the diner. My clients walked in and ask if I would like a tour before we went over the paperwork. They walked me around showed me where they sit for dinner, a small tour of their room and then they walked me to the room where they have Bible study. My client mentioned how much he enjoyed the Bible study.

They were so joyful and friendly to everyone there. I was so overwhelmed with how they were already so happy and comfortable in this new space. We sat and went over the paperwork and they said they hoped the family loved the home as much as they had all those years. The closing day came, and their son brought them to the closing. In this next moment, I really saw God's presence. During our closing, the title closer was starting the paperwork. My clients started asking questions and started conversing with the closer. They shared with her how they had just moved to their new assisted living home. She then opened up to how the last few months have been tough with her own father.

You see, her father's health was declining, and she was struggling with moving him to a nursing home. The closer shared some of her dad's story and all he went through recently. As the closing continued, and we neared the end of the paperwork, my clients asked if she would please write her father's name down on a piece of paper. They told her they had a list of people written down that they prayed for daily. They wanted to add her father to the list. She was overwhelmed with emotions, and so was I. God used these people, on this day, to bless this woman. Even though my clients were going through their own "new normal" and dealing with their health, they were prayer warriors, and this is what they do. When I left that closing, I knew God had placed them in my path, and the path of the closer.

*"In all things God works for the good of those who love Him,
who have been called according to His purpose."*
- Romans 8:28

Another touching recollection of a client being put in my path was during my own time of need. I have always held "open houses" during my real estate career. They are something I enjoy, giving me the opportunity of being face to face and meeting new people. During this particular open house, I talked to this family and spoke with their grandkids. Their former house recently went under contract in another state and they were just beginning the process here with a new home. They were familiar with the neighborhood and had always loved the location. After the open house, I followed up with a few answers to questions they had on that particular home. Due to the size of their family, they decided to look for a larger home, and we started our working relationship together.

With our ongoing visits to homes and conversations along the way, I got to know them and their family. Their grandkids started talking and were excited to see me each time we looked at different homes. I quickly started to connect with them. We eventually started talking about our faith and our church families. Both during the home inspection of their new home, and appraisal, we prayed together for each situation and outcome. We shared stories and began a friendship. Right before we were to close on this home for them, my husband lost his job. We talked and she immediately began to pray for him. Each time we texted or talked, she would ask about his job search and continued to pray.

By the time we got to the closing table, he had accepted a new job. She said they would continue to pray for us. This was such a blessing to us as we hadn't shared the news with many people and she was there by my side, cheering us on and praying for our family. Even though she was thanking me for helping them find their perfect home, I was thanking her for being such a prayer warrior. We both knew God had placed the path for us to meet and we continue to talk and pray for each other still today.

" For where two or three are gathered in my name,
there am I among them."
- Matthew 18:20

This last recollection speaks to looking for the signs God gives us and being aware of them. You see, this family needed to downsize. They put their home on the market and within a week it was under contract. They were so excited and immediately started packing boxes. However, there were a few unexpected obstacles with the sale. During one of the meetings at their home, the seller was feeling defeated. We talked about God's plans and timing. She trusted that God was taking care of things, even though to her and in this moment, it didn't make sense. We headed out of her home and into the garage. I turned back to her and to tell her goodbye. When I glanced over my shoulder in her garage, there was a chalkboard.

We have traveled through this garage many times, yet this was the first time I had seen the chalkboard. When I read what it said, I told her, "This is just what we need to see and there it was in the garage." They had written, "Have an attitude of gratitude." She remarked that we need to practice much more often, and we both agreed. She knew those words showed up as she was doubting the outcome of the sale. It all worked out, in fact, the timing was perfect. Their new home will be completed in the same time frame as to when their existing home is to be sold. God blessed us both that day.

"Do not let your hearts be troubled. Trust in God;
trust also in me."
- John 14:1

I hope you find these words, and the stories they create, to be of encouragement to you. Remember, you are fearfully and wonderfully made with a great purpose. Set the standard. Don't be like everyone else. Follow the leadership of the Holy Spirit. Love should be our main theme. Love God, Love ourselves, and Love other people. Do this and you will be given a heart like Jesus–given a gift of awareness. Listen intently and add value to others' lives wherever possible. We are doing God's work.

This is my calling and my purpose. When we listen to our clients and become part of their family, we help them achieve and receive their objectives. I believe the house they buy is different than any other house they would have bought had they worked with someone else. This starts with friends they make, families they touch with their life story. I believe we affect other people's lives and I believe this is my calling to serve God. In this way, I can use my gifts to help other people get what they want and need. Sometimes, we even help them through a healing process. Sometimes, we just listen. Sometimes, we knit our gifts with other brothers and sisters in Christ, to blanket their paths.

Those houses we sell, are homes we impact! Let me say that again, those houses we sell, are homes we impact! We are helping people with possibly their biggest investment. Shouldn't we invest in them? It is not through our success that God saves the world, but through our sacrifices. He calls us first to an altar, not a platform. I pray you seek God's word to find your transformation. I pray you seek his guidance through prayer. Praise him! Give him the

Glory! Show an Attitude of Gratitude in all things! Being a real estate agent is not about real estate; it is about relationships! Walk in Faith and Trust in Him. We want our clients to see delight in God. Grace & Peace!

"From the fullness of His grace, we have all received one blessing after another."
- John 1:16

How To Build Your Faith

1.What am I seeking? Where do I find joy and light?

_____

_____

_____

_____

_____

2. What I am Striving for? Who do you want to impact in the coming year? Are my actions in alignment?

_____

_____

_____

_____

_____

3. What is my value? Can you think of a time in your life when your words encouraged, comforted someone? How can you make a difference?

_____

_____

_____

_____

_____

4. What do you want your legacy to be? What did you deposit in the lives of people you came in contact with?

_____

_____

_____

_____

About Melissa Carpenter

Melissa Carpenter has been a REALTOR® for eighteen plus years. She has been a top agent in the Greater Cincinnati Ohio Area. She has an immense passion for mentoring agents in her industry. Melissa has shared her skills by volunteering on committees for years.

Outside of real esate, she gives time to a program called Upward. Melissa is a cheer commissioner for this cheerleading program. Not only are these things important to her, her family time is highly valued, as well.

Melissa loves spending time with her husband, Bryan. They have three children, two daughters-in-law, and one grandson. She absolutely adores her time with her family. Also, she enjoys walks and gardening, along with time spent at the lake.

Contact Melissa

- Website: www.MelissaCarpenter.com
- Email: Melissa@MelissaCarpenter.com

✝

Chapter 5
Miracles in the Ashes

BY JEN MAINS

It was a Monday in April. We were beginning to see the first glimpses of Spring as the snow melted and temperatures were climbing above freezing. This particular Monday was overcast, rainy, and blustery. We had just come out of a storm-filled weekend. Even with the gloomy weather, people were filled with anticipation of the changing season after experiencing our long, Minnesota winter.

On Mondays, I was privileged to coach the top agents in my company. And so, every 30 minutes back to back on Monday afternoons, I would have different agents meeting with me to discuss their business goals for the week. Those meetings made Mondays a favorite day of my week. It was the day when I enjoyed strengthening my relationships with those I was so privileged to be in business with. My agents were achieving great things; surpassing their goals month after month, even while some were facing great challenges – each had their own story to tell.

After all my meetings were done for the day, I was able to check messages and reply to all emails. At 4:20, I picked up my phone to see that I had missed six calls from my youngest son's cell phone. Ben was 15 and didn't like getting sent to my voicemail, so he would repeatedly call until I answered. So, seeing six missed calls from him wasn't too much of a surprise. However, little did I know, the voicemail that was left after the sixth call attempt was going to change my entire world forever.

As I began to listen, I heard my youngest daughter's voice screaming in panic. The wind was blowing so loudly through the phone, I had difficulty deciphering her words. I could hear her running footsteps as she screamed with each breath, "Mom, the house is on fire. We are out, but the house is burning. Mom, there's fire everywhere. Mom, everything is gone!" And then, the phone went dead.

At that moment time stood still. Everything got very quiet. I didn't notice any sights, sounds, and I don't recall having any thoughts, except disbelief. In those few seconds, everything stopped. I do distinctly remember thinking... "Wait – how did Ayden get Ben's phone?" Immediately, I dialed the number. It went directly to voicemail. I called my oldest son, Charlie's phone. Went directly to voicemail. Called my youngest daughter, Ayden's phone. Went directly to voicemail. Called my husband, Jim's phone. Went directly to voicemail. Called our oldest daughter, Haley's phone. Went directly to voicemail. At this point, I didn't know the condition of my family or my house. I ran out the door of my office and raced towards home.

Coming up to our neighborhood there was a sheriff blocking the street leading to our home. A line of cars had formed as he was checking everyone's identification before letting them pass. Driving up to his post, I opened my window as he leaned in to ask for my license and address. Irritated, I responded that it was my house burning down and to please get out of my way. He insisted, and after showing him my license, stated that I was the third person who told him it was their house on fire. Reluctantly he let me through. Later, his comment would make sense because my mother, brother, and aunt had all arrived upon the scene sooner than I did. You see, my house had been in my family since 1937; starting as a cabin, then becoming a home, which my grandparents owned. They sold it to my aunt and uncle, who sold it to my dad and mom, who sold it to me. Entire generations were raised in our little home on Tanner's Lake. Over 75 years of memories were created there.

Our home was located down on the lake and was not visible from the street. Fire trucks lined each side of the road, blocking all traffic from getting through. I parked in a neighbor's driveway and started walking towards our garage. In the distance, standing in the middle of the street, I saw Jim wearing shorts, a tee shirt, and cowboy boots that had been given to him from a neighbor. As I got closer, Jim walked over, hugged me and said, "It's all gone, hon. Everything is gone." He smelled of smoke and burned metal. The thought of that stench makes me nauseous even to this day. He assured me that he was fine. The kids were alright and had all managed to get out of the house, along with the dogs. We walked over to the garage and looked down at our home. Thick, black smoke was coming from all the windows and we could feel the heat all the way up on the street. It was completely engulfed in flames.

People often say that things are just things. And they're right. Material possessions are temporal and can be erased in a matter of minutes. The devastating part about losing our home was not the material possessions. The devastating part was losing the physical landmarks that had memories attached to them. It was the one place on this earth that I could sit in the exact same chair, on the exact same deck, and look out at the same lake that Dad and I would spend hours watching together. It was the same house with sloped floors in the kitchen and the squeaky staircase leading up to our bedrooms. With light switches that Dad had installed upside down. The same house that held thousands of guests through the years for our annual New Year's Day Skating Party. The same house that Dad would lock me out of, when I broke curfew. The same house HIS dad would lock him out of, when he broke curfew. It wasn't just a house. It was the foundation of our family, an integral part of our heritage. It was the place dearly beloved by my entire family and those friends who grew up as family under our roof. And it was the last place where my childhood memories of Dad still lived. A dad that was larger than life. A dad that was my hero. See, Dad was diagnosed with Pancreatic Cancer on January 21st, 2011. The doctors gave him 3-6 months to live. After fighting valiantly, Dad went to heaven to get his healing on February 17th, 2012. Standing in the detached garage, just two short years later watching black, thick smoke come from the broken-out windows of my home, I remember thinking how sad Dad would be if he saw it.

The fire started in the basement. The wind gusts that day fueled the fire into an intensity that quickly filled the entire lower level of our home. Within minutes, the entire basement and main levels were completely engulfed in flames. While Jim and Charlie did their best to fight the flames, their efforts were futile as the fire grew and the heat was too much for them to endure. Ben and Ayden grabbed our dogs and ran out of the home. Jim and Charlie followed behind. It was only after they were safely away from the house that they realized in the chaos they had forgotten to put on shoes. Barefoot, and with just the clothes on their backs, they watched all of our earthly possessions go up in flames.

We gathered inside of our garage and just watched and waited. We didn't know what else to do. People were so kind. Neighbors came with blankets, boots, coats, and lawn chairs. My agents started showing up with necessities and toiletries. Others came with food and hot coffee. Many who had been part of our home's history came. Extended family, friends from the past, current friends, and complete strangers all joined us. The kindness was overwhelming – such a mixture of gratitude and complete loss, all rolled into one night.

As the evening went on, more fire companies came to fight the fire. With the weather conditions and high winds, there was concern that our neighbor's homes may also catch fire. It became apparent that they were not going to be able to save our home, so their focus turned to containing the fire from doing more damage. We had been getting periodic updates from the Fire Captain, Kevin. As the night wore on, he asked to speak with Jim and me separately from the others. Directly, and with kindness, he proceeded to tell us that our home was a complete loss and they were unable to save the structure. He then asked, "Is there anything of value that I could try to retrieve for you?" My mind went immediately back to Dad.

When Dad passed away, Mom had given a few things to me and my brothers that she knew we would want. I was given the box of Dad's sermon notes and his Bible. Years of sermon notes scratched on random pieces of paper. None of them were in any organized fashion, whatsoever. Tattered pages which were illegible to many, yet I loved them because they were in his handwriting and I could almost hear his voice as I read them. They were his personal, most intimate thoughts and words that God had spoken to him to minister. His Bible included a poem that my Grandmother had written to him after he left the professional world of hockey to pursue his calling to be a minister. That poem was one of the most important things possessed by Dad. For a Christmas present one year, I had it laminated to preserve it from deteriorating. He kept that poem in the back-right-hand side of his Bible cover. He had years and years of notes etched in the margins of his Bible from previous sermons he had heard, or from sermons he had delivered himself. There were loose pages and the cover was almost completely separated from its binding. Corners were tattered and there were a few pages torn from the many years of use. His reading glasses were hooked inside the case. It had become one of my most precious and valued possessions.

Hoping for the slightest chance that it might be still recoverable, I asked Kevin to please save Dad's Bible and told him exactly where he could find it on the nightstand next to my bed. Our master bedroom was located on the third floor and so we weren't sure it was safe for anyone to go up there. The fire had burned so long and so hot that the floor joists and supports were compromised. Kevin kindly nodded his head and replied, "I'll see what I can do."

About thirty minutes later, he was back. I won't forget the scene. I was sitting in a lawn chair and wrapped in a blanket given to me from a neighbor. It was miserably cold, wet, and windy that night. In shock and freezing, I was shivering uncontrollably. Kevin appeared just outside the garage. A cloud surrounded him as smoke still drifted from his gear. He had his helmet still on, so I couldn't see his face. Walking towards me, arms stretched out directly in front of him, he was tenderly holding the most precious thing I wanted at that moment. He gently leaned down and handed me – Dad's Bible.

Steam and smoke was still coming from its case. The heat had started to melt the leather, yet, the zipper still worked. I opened the case, and it was all intact. The pages were not singed, the laminated poem was still tucked safely in the right-hand pocket. Dad's glasses were still clipped to the inside cover. Relief, disbelief, joy, and grief all filled my heart, simultaneously. I began to cry. Not just the sniffle-one-tear-streaming-down-your-face cry. Nope! I began to cry the ugly-bawl-your-eyes-out cry. I hadn't shed a tear yet – until then.

It was the only thing that they retrieved that night and it was the most precious thing in the world to me. To me, it was a piece of Dad. Amongst all the loss and devastation that came to my family that night, we also had peace. We were alive and we were safe. Near midnight, Kevin told us we didn't need to stay any longer. The fire had been extinguished and they would keep a small crew there overnight in case any hot spots reignited. Exhausted, freezing, numb, and in shock we left; never to spend another day inside of our dearly loved, memory-filled home. That day will forever be a moment that changed our family's life. It was April 28th, 2014.

The next morning our family and my Mom met Kevin and the Fire Marshal at the house to assess the damage. We were able to walk through the portions of the home that had not been demolished by the firefighters. The entire basement was unrecognizable.

There was nothing in it, and we could not go down into it. The main level looked like a bomb had gone off. The ceilings were torn down, insulation was everywhere. Holes had been cut in the floor to put out hot spots. Even though it was daylight, it was black as night inside the house. The windows were all covered with plywood and everything was charred. Kevin led us upstairs to our bedrooms which were not burned. The upper level was destroyed by water, heat, and smoke, however, the flames had not reached up there. We were told we could take items if we found them intact, so we all went into our rooms with flashlights and started to look. It was hard to breathe – the smoke and chemicals in the air burned our lungs, noses, eyes, and mouths. It was something we had never experienced, and we needed to frequently take shifts going outside for fresh air.

There was one more thing that I needed to retrieve. I had hoped beyond all logic that my Dad's box of sermon notes would be saved. Now mind you, his notes were written on paper and stored in an unsealed cardboard box. Not inside of plastic Tupperware or something durable – they were in an open, cardboard box. I could not find it anywhere. I knew that I had initially put it in a spot away from everyday traffic for safe-keeping and yet I couldn't remember for the life of me where I stashed it. Then it hit me!! I had stored it under my bed.

Every surface in our room was wet, scorched, or melted. The lamps, nightstands, and bed were melted into one large mess. Our bedspread was melted to the pillows and mattress. The intense heat had turned everything into liquid;

melting it all together. I crawled along the side of my bed, reaching underneath to pull out the box; not knowing what I would find. Unbelievably I pulled out a completely untouched, unsinged, un-melted, fully-intact cardboard box filled with paper, handwritten notes. Cardboard and paper – completely unharmed by the water, smoke, and intense heat that had melted every other thing inside of our room.

More treasures were found that day...from the kids finding their autographed copies of Dad's autobiography with messages that he personally wrote to each of them...to their personal Bibles...to the scorecard that Charlie had kept from the last time he played golf with his Grandpa...to the book shelf that was made from a ski that Dad had designed from the waterski company he owned. Yes, we had lost 99% of everything we owned that day, yet we were blessed that the dearest things had been spared. Our hearts were grateful.

Years later as I write this chapter, I can clearly see God's hand protecting us, keeping us, and guiding us even in the darkest times. Miracle after miracle occurred. The kindness shown to Jim, the kids, and me from our family, our church family, our friends, co-workers, business partners, and complete strangers was like nothing I had seen before. We received gift cards from real estate professionals across the country – Ziploc bags stuffed with gift cards. Friends set up a Go-Fund-Me page where people from all over the world donated. Leaders from within my Keller Williams company called, sent texts and notes of encouragement to our family. Funds from our KW Cares Charitable Organization were donated into our account before midnight on the night of the fire. A locally-owned, family restaurant provided meals to our family for an entire year while we rebuilt. When we asked them to please allow us to pay, the owner and our friend Ed would reply, "Our kitchen is your kitchen until you have a kitchen." God's goodness was revealed to us through precious, overwhelming human kindness. My Mom opened the lower level in her home, allowing us to move in for a month while we searched for temporary housing. One of my dear friends was able to locate and negotiate a rental home for us in a beautiful neighborhood. Another friend, and local builder, graciously agreed to demolish our current home and custom design and build our new home.

Miracle after miracle continued - like the cherished, sentimental things that were salvaged from the fire miraculously unscathed. God knew how precious these things were to us and He graciously spared them from destruction. He cares that much for us. The timing of the fire was at 4:00 in the afternoon when everyone was awake. Had it happened at night, Kevin and the Fire Marshal were sure there would have been 6 deaths associated with this fire. Our house fire never hit the news. It is unheard of and yet we had no local media attention. We had no risk of anyone taking advantage of the situation because no one knew about it outside those near us. God protected us. He kept us. He hid us. He provided for us. He made a way for us.

God makes paths for each of us in ways we cannot see. He knows the beginning from the end. He has established plans for situations far before we even know they are going to happen.

"And we know that all things work together for good to them that love God, to them who are the called according to his purpose."
- Romans 8:28

I never really understood that verse to the extent that I do now. Things that seem so utterly horrible actually are working together for our good. Not to make us feel good, rather, they are working together for our benefit – for our good and for His glory.

You see, the greatest miracle of this story we hadn't even experienced yet. Two days after the fire, we met our insurance representative, Christina, at a Caribou Coffee near our house to go through our homeowner's insurance policy. While reviewing the report received from the fire chief, I couldn't hold back the tears as we relived the previous 48 hours. We went through detailed information on how the fire started, how it grew, what was destroyed, and that our insurance company, too, agreed it was a complete loss.

Noticing my emotions, Christina gently leaned over and touched my hand. She started, "Mr. and Mrs. Mains, I am so sorry for your loss. I have reviewed the information in your policy and ran it through my supervisor for confirmation. I had to run it through upper management because I was surprised to see the details of your particular policy. You see, it is very unique. We haven't issued this type of policy in all the years I have been working for our company. Your policy states that upon your home being deemed a complete loss, our company will cover all costs associated with the rebuild and payoff the outstanding mortgage on your current home. This coverage encompasses the demolition and removal of the all damaged structures, the design and rebuilding of a new home, all costs associated with temporary housing and all fixtures needed for housing including rental furniture, linens, dishes, household items - from carpets to trash cans – all of it is covered. Upon rebuilding, all costs associated with the new home, new landscaping, retaining walls, driveway and sidewalks are all covered. I have never in all my years seen this type of policy." Jim and I sat in disbelief. And then we remembered...

Twenty years prior, when James and I were first married and living in an apartment, my Dad introduced us to a kind, older man named Don. Don was my Dad's and Mom's insurance provider who owned a State Farm Insurance franchise. Dad was insistent that we only use Don for our insurance. And so, we met with him to discuss our current renters needs and any future possible homeowners' needs. Jim and I distinctly remember Don telling us "Kids, I want you to purchase this insurance policy, and never let it lapse. It seems a bit higher than what you could find for a simple renter's policy, but I don't want you to ever let this policy go. Never change it or move into another policy – just keep this one." We had no idea what we were doing. We just trusted my Dad, we trusted Don, and we did what he told us. Every time we would get a piece of mail offering a new insurance policy, Jim would throw it away. He never forgot that conversation with Don over twenty years ago. Each time we moved; we kept our policy with Don. When Don retired, we kept our policy with Maggie, Don's predecessor at the same company. Little did we know, but God knew. He had it planned perfectly.

"'For I know the plans I have for you,' declares the LORD, 'plans to prosper you and not to harm you, plans to give you hope and a future.'"
– Jeremiah 29:11

As you are reading this, you might be in a season of trial. You might be on a journey where it seems so very dark. You may feel abandoned, lost, hopeless, and full of fear. I encourage you to find the miracles in your darkness. See the good things He is doing. Notice the miracles that are being orchestrated that you may not even know are occurring. Trust Him. He holds us in the palm of His hand. He knows, He hears, He cares. And He is making ways in the wilderness and streams in the desert. Trust Him, on this one; He will bring beauty from ashes.

Journey on, my friends and do not grow weary. Your miracle may be in the fire.

How To Build Your Faith

1. What does trusting in Him mean to you?

_____

_____

_____

_____

_____

2. Has there ever been a time when you felt alone in a dark season? In I Samuel 30:6, scripture tells us that David encouraged himself in the LORD. What does this scripture mean to you?

_____

_____

_____

3. When facing trials, what can you do to encourage yourself in the LORD? What strategies can you implement that would help you keep yourself encouraged?

_____

_____

_____

_____

_____

4. What can you do to be more purposeful about noticing the daily miracles He works on your behalf?

_____

_____

_____

_____

_____

About Jen Mains

Jen has worked in the real estate industry for over 24 years. She has been an active sales agent, built, run, and coached top-producing real estate teams, and has served as a Team Leader of three different Keller Williams Market Centers over the span of 12 years.

Jen finds great fulfillment in coaching real estate professionals from coast to coast as they grow their businesses, attract and lead talent to their teams, and build wealth through implementing systems while creating balance in their lives. A highly motivated leader with excellent communication and problem-solving skills, she is driven to succeed and inspires others to reach their highest potential.

Outside of work, Jen and her husband, James, pastor a church in Woodbury, MN. There she leads worship, writes, and teaches Bible studies.

When not leading her real estate office, coaching her agents, or leading worship in church, Jen spends her time fulfilling the most significant role of her life: Wife to James and Mom of their four beautiful children - the most important people in her life.

Contact Jen

- Website: www.JenMains.com
- Email: CoachJenMains@Gmail.com
- Phone: 651-775-8493

✝

Chapter 7

From Homeless to Freedom

BY J. MICHAEL MANLEY

When I started in real estate back in 2003, I started because I had another company that lost a major contract and had to close. Real estate was suggested to me by a family member as a way to start over. Always up for a challenge, I said 'ok' and started school in December of 2002, and was licensed on January 15th, 2003.

I was excited, nervous, and desperate to earn income. I remember my Broker In Charge telling me to call For Sale By Owners and Expired listings. It worked, and my second year I sold 42 homes! I was on cloud nine and even being recruited by a local prestigious company. I made the switch and continued to work hard and earn an amazing income. The world according to my perspective was awesome; I was making great income, was married, had my first son, Colin, and in a new home. That was until…it wasn't amazing anymore.

I was working all of the time! Vacation–working…weekends– working…nights–working! I came from a family that work ethic was highly praised, and I was following the model laid out for me, by my own family.

My wife, at the time, was raised differently. Her dad had worked for the same company and had earned numerous weeks of vacation. He made a great income, and when he was off of work, he was off. Things for us as a family started great, until being in real estate meant that I never stopped working. 2007 was the best year in the real estate industry since I had started, however I missed out on it, working with challenges in my marriage. Needless to say, we separated and eventually divorced.

The market was shifting, and I was no longer able to afford the new home we had purchased. The shift in 2008 ripped the rug out from under me. I sold the home two weeks before it was to be sold on the courthouse steps, staving off a foreclosure. Yet now, my son and I were living in an apartment, barely making ends meet. This began the start of a VERY long journey for me to turn back to God and started living the life he had planned for me.

"For I know the plans and thoughts that I have for you," says the LORD, "plans for peace and well-being and not for disaster, to give you a future and a hope."
- Jeremiah 29:11

Later in 2007, I met a lady named Vicki from work. We began talking, started dating, and we married in December of 2008. I didn't realize it at the time, yet God had brought Vicki into my life to help guide me with getting my life in order. Vicki was in real estate and knew the work ethic that real estate required, and her parents were long time salespeople. I felt she understood the work ethic I had been living and loved me, not in spite of, but rather because of my work habits. She had gone through a divorce as well. We both love God, and knew God had placed us together.

In early 2009, I was out running one Saturday, and praying and begging God to tell me what he desired me to do to earn income for our family. My idea was to follow leads in order to generate a new "real job" (I hate that term, now). That day I audibly heard God tell me this was my Garden of Gethsemane. I didn't really know what that meant. I went home to google it and it hit me. This was where Jesus went to before he fulfilled his destiny. When Vicki came home that day, I told her what God had spoken to me. She immediately was scared, and I didn't really know why. She said that is where Jesus went to pray before he was arrested! She was like, "you are getting ARRESTED!!!" I did my best to reassure her that I didn't believe that was it! This was just the pain I was going through to reshape my character to be able to fulfill my destiny!

In April of 2009, things got worse. One day while my mother-in-law was at the house, our power was turned off because we didn't have the $69 to pay the power company. Thus, Vicki and I made the decision to move in with her parents to help us get back on our feet! I don't believe either of us realized the many blessings God provided at the time while we were living there! We both just wanted to get up on our feet, and buy a home of our own. I truly believe God was using this time to break any ego I had, to allow me to die to myself, and see His plan.

"I assure you, believers, by the pride which I have in you in [your union with] Christ Jesus our Lord, I die daily [I face death and die to self]."
- 1 Corinthians 15:31

In April of 2009, I switched to a new brokerage–Keller Williams Realty, and started rebuilding my business. My team leader, Tommy Stevenson, asked me to take a class that was coming to the market center called BOLD. I didn't have the money to attend, yet figured out how to make it happen. I jumped in feet first so I could build to a level so that I could move Vicki into a new home, that she deserved. This class was about mindset and things I had never heard of before. It was very weird, yet I felt like God was speaking to me in each class. I took the principles they were teaching back to the word of God and found scriptures that matched up with what they were teaching. This was the first time I really felt like life was enough to walk in amazing peace, expectancy, and abundance!

"For we are His workmanship (His own master work, a work of art), created in Christ Jesus (reborn from above—spiritually transformed, renewed, ready to be used) for good works, which God prepared (for us) beforehand (taking paths which He set), so that we would walk in them (living the good life which He prearranged and made ready for us)."
- Ephesians 2:10

During this time, I realized that the devil had had spiritual strongholds on my mind that were keeping me from walking in God's peace and provision He had for my family and I. BOLD, which stands for a Business Objective a Life by Design, isn't a spiritual God-focused course, yet, the principles were definitely aligning with God's Word. My life was starting to transform. In 2011, we purchased our own home and were able to move out of my in-laws' home. Life was moving along. We had an amazing family, a beautiful home, and God blessed us with another son, Grayson; Vicki's first child of her own. Life was awesome!

My business was flourishing and our marriage was great as I had learned how to work/life counterbalance. In 2012, we had our third son, Pearson. Then in 2015, I had an opportunity to become a coach and teach BOLD. This would be a challenging period for our family as I would spend long days on the road traveling away from the family. Vicki, being left alone to handle the family's daily needs alone. Vicki and I discussed the challenges and prayed, seeking God's direction, putting Him first in our lives. We decided to do it, and off to Austin, Texas I went to audition. There were two days of auditioning. The first day was to see who was committed, and the second day we were to present individually on two different topics. On the second day, about seven of the people who were there the first day had already quit. It was my turn to present on my first topic, and I froze! I literally forgot all of the words and completely blanked! Oh no! Had Vicki and I not heard God correctly? I knew I had studied and knew the material, yet I was still attempting to be in control. At lunch I turned it over to God and prayed for his will to be done. I became unattached to the outcome and placed it all on God. The second section I was to present was on For Sale By Owners. This was the section I had studied, yet, not as much as the first section. It was my turn to present, I handed it to God and started. I really don't remember much about my presentation. It just happened, and at the end I remember thinking that was awesome! That feeling was confirmed when the person in charge said, "That is how a professional does it!" I became a BOLD coach!

"Therefore, put on the complete armor of God, so that you will be able to [successfully] resist and stand your ground in the evil day [of danger], and having done everything [that the crisis demands], to stand firm [in your place, fully prepared, immovable, victorious]."
- Ephesians 6:13

During the next several years, Vicki and I really started studying the Bible together and got clarity on the principle of success in the Kingdom of God. In the summer of 2018, God revealed that the process he had taken me through had put me on this path of living out Jeremiah 29:11.

In this section, let me break down what God revealed:

The freedom that I had received from the strongholds of the devil over my mind clearly followed a process set forth by God. There are three parts to this roadmap that anyone can follow: Forgiveness, Belief, and Faith.

Forgiveness- This is the foundation of the Bible; it is the basis for the entire Christ-followers' plan. In Matthew 18:21-35, Jesus tells the story of the Unforgiving Servant. In this story there is a servant of the king that owes the king 10,000 talents (about 200,000 years of pay). The servant begs the king for forgiveness and the king grants forgiveness of the debt. What an amazing king to allow such! The parable goes on to say the servant goes and finds his own servant that owes 100 Denali (about 4 months of wages) and demands he pay his debt. He even goes as far as to choke him, the Bible explains. When the people around saw this, they reported it to the king. The king called his servant in, that he had forgiven this massive amount of debt. He said, "I have forgiven you of so much, you should have forgiven your servant." The king turned the man over to the jailers to be tormented until he paid the debt he owed. According to the Roman law, at the time, if he couldn't pay the debt, he would be sold into slavery. This is the equivalent to God's forgiveness of our sins, and then us holding unforgiveness towards others! We are then turned over to the tormenter to be a slave, as we can never repay the debt for what Christ has done for us! That slavery happens in our minds allowing the devil to torment us daily when we hold unforgiveness of others! I believe once we have accepted Christ into our life, we must walk in forgiveness as Christ has forgiven us. Meaning not just for our past sins, but also for our future sins as well. Are you walking in your life in forgiveness for the past, and the future? Are you holding offense that you need to let go?

This is the first thing we must do to live a Jeremiah 29:11 life.

The second part of the roadmap is Belief. The Bible tells us in Mark 11:23-24, the parable of the sower.

"I assure you and most solemnly say to you, whoever says to this mountain, 'Be lifted up and thrown into the sea!' and [does not doubt in his heart [in God's unlimited power], but believes that what he says is going to take place, it will be done for him [in accordance with God's will]. For this reason I am telling you, whatever things you ask for in prayer [in accordance with God's will], believe [with confident trust] that you have received them, and they will be given to you."

I love this verse in the Amplified version because it speaks of God's unlimited power in accordance to God's will and trusting with confidence. Let's take God's will. This one thing trips most people up and keeps them from living the plan God has for them. For figuring out God's will we turn to Proverbs 16:3.

"Commit your works to the Lord (submit and trust them to Him), And your plans will succeed (if you respond to His will and guidance)."
- Proverbs 16:3

The Bible says commit YOUR plans to the Lord and YOUR

plans will succeed. Your plans are God's will when you commit them to the Lord. Meaning not doing them for selfish reasons, doing them for the Lord! That is powerful when you realize that God gave you these plans and He desires you to accomplish them! Many people have a challenge when they start doing something. We mostly doubt–Is this is what God desires me to do? Will God bless this action/goal? This is doubt! Exactly what God tells us not to do! God is looking for us to take action in the direction of a goal, and then rely on Him to guide our steps. Knowing that he may not give a straight path to follow, and seeking Him first in each step. In practice, this is looking and praying for God to bring the right people to you. Praying before hiring an assistant, to gain peace from God, before hiring them. Even praying before setting your yearly goals, gaining peace, and then moving forward with 100% belief.

This is the second thing we must do to live a Jeremiah 29:11 life.

The third part of this roadmap is Faith. Faith, many of you may be asking, isn't that the same thing as belief? According to the Bible they are similar, yet, they are used in different ways. When the Bible speaks of Faith it is mostly asking people to take action. Faith is an action verb, as found in James 2:22.

"You see that [his] faith was working together with his works, and as a result of the works, his faith was completed [reaching its maturity when he expressed his faith through obedience]."
- James 2:22

God desires us to take action and make sure we are moving forward. Faith through obedience and action, as if you are working for the Lord. Are you taking action like you are working for the Lord? That is such a powerful question to judge if your actions enough and right with integrity.

Using this roadmap can ensure you live a Jeremiah 29:11 life. In the Lord's prayer we are given insight for our life to live.

"Your kingdom come, Your will be done On earth as it is in heaven."
- Matthew 6:10

As with an actual roadmap, if we follow the directions, we will reach our goals. If we ignore even street, we will not reach our goal. The best part about the roadmap is if we make a wrong turn, we have a roadmap that allows us to adjust and get back on track.

How To Build Your Faith

1. What has God placed on your heart for a goal?

_____

_____

_____

_____

_____

2. Have I committed my goals to God?

_____

_____

_____

3. Do you believe with 100% confidence?

_____

_____

_____

_____

_____

4. What are you doubting? Have you taken it to God and gotten peace from the Holy Spirit?

_____

_____

_____

_____

_____

5. What actions do you need to take today to move forward?

_____

_____

_____

_____

_____

6. Are you taking action as if working for the Lord?

_____

_____

_____

_____

_____

About J. Michael Manley

J. Michael Manley is a Christ-following husband to his wife Vicki and father to his three boys Colin, Grayson, and Pearson. He grew up in a church that had little grace for people. In his search for God's direction in his life, he has grown in understanding and friendship with Christ.

J. Michael has been a REALTOR® since 2003. The shift of the market in 2008, led him to strengthen his walk with Christ. Since 2008, he has established a mega agent team in the Upstate of SC, started a profitable real estate photography company–Carolina House Shots, and became a coach for other businesses and individuals. These companies are God's companies, and God allows J. Michael to lead them for now as he guides people to live their Jeremiah 29:11 life.

Contact J. Michael

- Facebook: www.Facebook.com/JMichaelManley
- Linkedin: www.LinkedIn.com/in/JMichaelManley
- Instagram: www.Instagram.com/JMichaelManley

✝

Chapter 8

Not Your Typical Journey

BY AMANDA POWELL

In January of 2010, I took my first exam to become a real estate agent. I lived in Texas, at the time, and my husband was deployed. While having two small kids at home, I decided to pursue my real estate license, not knowing what all would come from it. I had the privilege of working in my hometown and helping families that were dear to my heart for ten months. I had the assistance of my mom helping with my two children, and the support of my husband from afar. This part of my career began in a town that I grew up in and with no more than 65,000 people. My office consisted of ten people who were amazing. These numbers are important because my next journey through real estate was very different.

My husband came home safely from another deployment and we moved to Kansas. Our family only lived in Kansas for 13 months. I spent that 13 months not doing real estate, but being involved in women's bible study, church, and my kids' activities. It was such an amazing time growing closer to God, having my husband home for the entire time, and making lifelong friends. Now in true military fashion, we didn't stay in Kansas long and the Army moved us to Maryland. We arrived January 31, 2012, and by May, I had my Maryland real estate license. Starting my career again in Maryland was very different. I did not know a single person in the state, I joined an office that had 400 people and worked five counties that had a combination of 2,807,353 people.

Moving never bothered me, but going into the unknown of my real estate journey was scary. After only being in Maryland for a few months, my husband left on another deployment, I finished my Bachelors degree, we moved to a new house and I sold my first house. The first family I was able to help in Maryland truly became a blessing in so many ways. They were the start of my journey in real estate in Maryland, bought the house next door and became some of our best friends. They were a huge support for me during the time my husband was deployed or traveling helping with my two children when I needed to work. God knew exactly who we needed in our lives and he put them right next door. Over the course of our seven years in Maryland, my husband was deployed or traveled for 4.5 years. This made for some long days, especially when work was busy, and kids kept me on my toes. Luckily, I did not have to rely on just me. I know where my strength comes from. My strength comes from God alone.

"God arms me with strength, and he makes my way perfect."
- Psalms 18:32

From the end of 2012 to 2018, our time was filled with sports, school, long hours helping real estate clients, and more deployments. My real estate journey has not been easy and is far from over, but so far I have had the honor of helping over 200 people buy, sell or rent a home. This is huge for me because it is more than just a number.

The majority of those people are active duty military members, or veterans. Helping military families has been so special for me, and real estate has allowed me to follow that passion. Before I got into real estate, my husband and I had bought and sold our first home. We had gone through the experience of purchasing, and then having to sell when the Army was ready to move us. Helping families in similar situations makes me so proud and thankful to do my part of assisting to make their transition to a new location a little smoother.

So many prayers have been said for clients, their families, their deals, my family, and coworkers. Having God to lean on when things were going smooth, as well as when they were hard and bumpy, really keeps me going. My hope is that everyone knows and feels God's love for them and the strength He can provide in personal life, and business. In 2018, my husband decided to retire from the Army. This came about in April, and by July, the kids and I were headed to Texas. He spent a few more months in Maryland until his leave started, but we wanted our kids to start their new school on time. The timeline was so short and we had so much to do. I was busy helping clients, packing a house, finding a new home in Texas, spending time with soon-to-be-missed friends, and figuring out how I would run my business from afar. I spent so many years building my business and relationships there that I did not want to give up everything I had worked for. While in Maryland, I worked at two brokerages and three offices. I can say that I was able to work and build relationships with so many amazing REALTOR®. I experienced personal and professional growth due to these wonderful people. This became very important when it came time to move. There was no way that I would have been able to continue my business from another state, alone. I definitely feel that God puts the people that you need in your life when you need them. This has been so true for me. Now that doesn't mean that we don't spend time with people that we shouldn't at times. When we are purposeful about those we give our time and energy to, great things can happen. Jim Rohn, renowned businessman and personal development guru, said: **"You are the average of the five people you spend the most time with."** I have found that remembering this can be important and help as growth and life happens.

Moving to Texas was exciting, and scary. Exciting because we were heading back near the place we grew up and would be around family and old friends. Scary because we were leaving the full-time careers and amazing relationships that we had built over six years in Maryland. The only way it was possible for me to move half-way across the country and continue with my business was with the help of my brokerage, a pair of phenomenal REALTOR®, and most importantly, God. Transition is never easy, especially when so much is unknown, but faith allows for strength and guidance through the known, and unknown. Having faith doesn't mean things will always go the way you want them to or that hard times won't come from circumstances, but it does reassure you that God is with you.

Moving, while having a real estate career, has allowed me to continue my growth journey. Learning to run a business from afar, learning to rely on others, and having gratitude through it all. I have been blessed to know many military spouses who have moved while having built careers, and one thing I always want to do is to continue to learn from others. One piece of advice I can give, whether you are working on personal or professional growth, is to never stop learning. Spend time with people who can pour into you, read books, listen to podcasts, attend events that are learning based, and never be afraid to ask questions, or for help.

As I continue on my growth and mindset journey, one thing

that I find sticks with me is that there are only two things we can control. The following quote I have found to be said in different ways by many people but it rings so true. "The **two things** in life **you** are in total **control** over are your **attitude** and your **effort**." - Billy Cox.

In business and life, things are not always easy, they don't go the way you want and you encounter people who are going through their own trials. Going through a real estate transaction can be very emotionally draining for the parties involved. Reminding myself in all situations that I can control my attitude and effort has allowed me to better deal with tough situations and let go of stress. Change in life and business can add to the stressors of life but going into it knowing you are fully in control of your attitude and effort, while leaning on God, I have found can allow for growth and peace. Remembering that everything we do is a choice is important. As I continue to run my business and follow my passions through real estate, and other ventures, I remind myself that I get to choose my attitude and effort. Make sure to remember as you are working towards anything you love in business and your personal life that you understand you get to choose. You get to choose how you act, react, and what you pour into your goals and dreams.

I recently got a tattoo that is small and simple, but to me has incredible meanings. Although tattoos are not always seen as appropriate in business settings, I have worked over the years to become more of who I want to be. While striving to do my best in my business, I have gotten over some of my thoughts on other people's opinions. I know not everyone will look at things the way I do, but I definitely think there are ways to express yourself and still be professional. This tattoo goes along so much with what this chapter is about. In tiny red letters on my wrist are the words "I AM." Why "I AM?" First it is my favorite name of God! That is why I fell in love with the idea of getting it to begin with. Then, for mindset it is an amazing reminder. I AM strong, confident, a great mom, a talented REALTOR®, I AM capable of anything, etc. Building a business, moving, having so much change, and reshaping yourself to be exactly who you want to be can all be done. Learn from those who strive for growth, be proud of your accomplishments, and trust that God will be with you all along the way.

How To Build Your Faith

1. What do you do on a daily, weekly, monthly and yearly basis to work on your mindset?

_____

_____

_____

_____

_____

2. Have you looked at your sphere lately? Do you spend time with people who make you strive to be better? Will those people be the ones to help you through change and growth?

_____

_____

_____

_____

3. How do you deal with stress and change?

_____

_____

_____

_____

_____

4. Are you following your passion and allowing your attitude and effort to reflect your goals?

_____

_____

_____

_____

_____

About Amanda Powell

Amanda Powell is the owner of The A Team of Keller Williams. She began her real estate career in 2010, in East Texas. After relocating to Maryland in early 2012, Amanda received her Maryland Real Estate license and began working for Long and Foster. Diving into helping families, Amanda was awarded Rookie of the Year in 2013, and Agent of the Year in 2014. Since 2013, she has received several designations and completed her Bachelor of Science, with a concentration in Marketing in the Fall of 2012.

Amanda specializes in helping military families relocate to and from all over the world to purchase and sell. Her goal is to make the PCS process as smooth as possible. Helping VA buyers be better prepared for the home purchasing process is important. Amanda also works hard for sellers with her extensive marketing knowledge and aggressive negotiation expertise.

Amanda understands the needs of military families as she is a military spouse. She has been married to her spouse for 17 years. Chris recently retired from the Army after being active duty for just over 20 years. Chris and Amanda have PCS'ed five times in their 17-year marriage. They have two children, Krystyne (14) and Christopher (12). In her free time, Amanda enjoys the gym and spending time with family and friends.

Contact Amanda Powell

- Website: www.TheATeamMD.com
- Email: Amanda@TheATeamMD.com
- Phone: 443-818-1299 - Cell
- Phone: 410-729-7700 - Office

✝

Chapter 9
My Turning Point

BY KELLIE RUTHERFORD

"You can have it all. Just not all at once."
- Oprah Winfrey

I remember waking up that morning and looking in the mirror. Seeing my reflection, I knew that I had to stop ruining myself, and yet, I couldn't stop. All I could think of was "I had no time for me." I had become one of those people working between 16 to 18 hours a day, 7 days a week. Feeling angry at the world at times because I knew my body wasn't feeling well, and at the same time I had such high demands from my clients. I was angry that I didn't have the empowerment to take care of me and put me first. The demand was so horrendous, and I felt I didn't have a choice.

Studying myself in the mirror, I knew I wasn't myself or in the right mindset. I justified that all the dizziness was because I was overworked, yet, I knew I brought that on myself. I kept asking myself "Do I continue at this pace?" I had nobody to help me.

This isn't what I really thought a real estate job was going to be like. I was looking at that aspect with fear more than anything, not knowing what was going on with me.

It wasn't something I was aware of at the time, but I was more self-reliant than relying on my faith that God will take care of me. At that time, I was struggling with a really unhealthy personal relationship and I was just so focused on "I can do this, I can do this." Instead of giving it over, and saying "Okay, what does God want for me? Will God help me through this?" I was not taking time off from work and putting myself to the bottom of the list, and my faith wasn't as strong as it had been years prior.

I had taken my eyes off my faith and started digging into the business. I was doing more, wanting to be more, and having more–instead of just being who I am.

I thought I was great.

I thought I had all the answers.

I thought my business was going good.

In achievement mode, I was doing a ton of business. There was a constant flow of business–but in the reality of it–I took eyes off of myself and what was best for me. You might say that I was killing myself, literally. Things had to change.

Looking back now, I count this realization, and change to stop doing such, as a blessing. Still to this day, as early as last week, I catch myself being tempted to go back to that mode of "work, work, work," instead of allowing natural abilities within myself to flow–not forcing it and letting go and letting God lead.

It might have been just me, but I had gotten caught up so much in the world of perception. Often there is a trap where what we want others to think about us takes such a priority that we forget to think about ourselves.

Moment of Truth

"The counsel of the Lord stands forever, and the plans of his heart to all generations."
– Psalm 33:11

Walking into work that day, I knew I had nothing more to give. I knew that something was drastically wrong. Yet, I wasn't wise enough to say "No more." I wasn't strong enough to say, "I come first." I was so worried and concerned about what the outcome would be if I dropped the ball on my client. I didn't want to let others down. Although I had gotten up that morning feeling scrawny and looking as bad as I did, I still pressed on. Even though I had that conversation with myself in the mirror, I chose to go in and act as if everything was okay. I felt like "I had to be on" for others.

Lupe, my broker, was the person that I needed in my life that day. I walked in the door. She told me that I looked like a ghost, and she demanded that I see a doctor. It was probably her that saved my life by telling me to let go and go take care of me. Even though there were times she and I didn't see eye to eye, she cared. She had the courage to tell me "Go do what you need to do for you." I am so very grateful for what she did that day. During my illness, her son was the one who stepped up and tremendously helped.

I did drop everything, as Lupe suggested. That day, I gave over everything I was supposed to do. It was absolute chaos. I was scared, I was afraid of what I didn't know.

I went over to see my primary doctor, I sat on the table. The doctor came up and said "Hey, apparently your vertigo is going a little bit haywire, let's just go ahead and put you on more prescriptions." I remember telling the doctor, "You know what, you aren't bothering to look over my chart. What the heck do you know about what's going on with me? We are done. I will go find another doctor." I had been born with a heart defect, and instinct within me took over. I walked out and he kept calling me to come back. I walked out thinking, this is my only life, something is not right.

I got into my car with tears streaming down my face and drove down to my office telling Lupe exactly what happened. She suggested I sit down while she called her own doctor, who lived about 47 miles away. I was in tears while she made the call and I agreed to go see her doctor. She asked me if I wanted her son, Scott to drive me. Stubborn, I said no because I needed to gain control, and not let someone else drive me.

Once I got to her doctor, Dawn, she sat there asking me tons of questions and ordered lots of tests. "I agree with Lupe, you are not looking good right now, you need to take some down time" she said.

I cried and told her that she didn't understand. Strongly she replied, "No, young lady, YOU don't understand—you need to let go." Sensing my concern, she continued, "I have known Lupe for a long time, she will have your back."

The very next day I went in for a nutritionist test—vitamins and everything in my blood looked fine. Nothing was showing up in the tests. It wasn't until after this seventh test, that the issue was revealed. Three days later, they ordered for a cardiologist to see me in Safford to do an ultrasound on my heart. I have had other ultrasounds in my life because I was born with a murmur. Thus, I was tested and followed until I was 22—a while ago. Having seen so many ultrasounds in my life, I knew immediately what I saw on that screen. It scared the living daylight out of me.

The doctor came back in and confirmed that something was going on. He commented "Well, the good thing is, you are in really good shape. The other good thing is, you are young. The thing we need to take care of now and make arrangements to do so is… young lady, I am going to need to open you up…going to need to crack your chest open. You've got a depleted aorta valve that I need to replace. Right now, you are living on about 30% of your blood. It's a wonder you have not had congestive heart failure already. It's a miracle you are still here. What are you going to do, are you going forward?"

I was silent, in shock, and then he asked "What are you doing for a living?"

I answered, "I am a REALTOR®." He retorted back, "You are done. Your work stops now because you have one of the highest stressful jobs that could possibly be out there for the condition in which you are in at this moment in time, is that understood? You are done!"

All I could do was cry "Yeah, I will do whatever I need to do."

Because He Lives, I Can Face Tomorrow

"Fear not, for I am with you; be not dismayed, for I am your God; I will strengthen you."
- Isaiah 41:10

This was when I finally gave myself permission to take care of me.

I didn't like the cardiologist's news, or his bedside manner. I wasn't comfortable. I knew I needed to have that sense of comfort with what I was about to go through. So, I went back the following week to choose another doctor for the actual surgery. I decided that I was going for the best, no matter the cost, since I had one heart, and one life.

Prior to the surgery, my blood pressure was sky high. The surgeon and the cardiologist both said "We can't operate on you, as much as we want. To do this now, we need to get your blood pressure down—we need to get you calm." They asked me further, "What are you doing to relax? What do you have planned for the summer that you enjoy?"

For the past 5 years, I would go deep sea fishing in Mexico with a group of people. The fishing trip was coming up soon. I was scheduled to leave June 11th, living for the next 14 days on a mother ship in Mexico with Pongas attached. After I told them of my plans, the doctors suggested I go on the trip and relax and rest.

The people that I had gone fishing with every year for the last five years would be going on this trip. In those five years, we *never* discussed our profession. Our motto was, "We leave our business at the shore!" We came together to enjoy the adventure of fishing.

On a particular day, I went up to the captain's galley. "Hey, what's going on?" he asked. I told him what was going on. He called in one of the guys we have been fishing with for years. I was slightly perturbed, asking "What is he doing here?"

"I know you guys agreed that nobody would know what you guys do for a living," he replied, "but you need to know this in order to give yourself peace and comfort—and relax. This person sitting right next to you is a cardiologist." I was blown away by hearing this because I knew God was taking care of me on this trip–his hand was on my life.

I went through that fishing trip. I rested. I slept a ton. I didn't fish that much because I had no energy. When I got back, I went in for my surgery. I can remember laying there and my family standing over me, and I said, "Don't worry, God is not done with me. He's got bigger things he wants me to do, I will be back." Not a tear was shed, instead there was a smile on my face–I knew that God was not done with me.

I remember *that* day. Walking out of the house to go for my surgery and turning around I looked around at my house and all the stuff in it. I wondered if I would be back. If when I did come back, if I would be different. I remember that day–like it was today. I will never forget how I looked at life then versus how I do today.

After the surgery, it was tough. I had to learn how to breathe again. I had to work on inflating my lungs. It hurt so much having to look at this huge scar. "Will I be appealing to somebody else with that kind of scar running down the middle of my chest?" But, at that time, immediately after the surgery, I didn't care about that. I was alive. I *chose* to learn. I had to learn how to walk and breathe.

Every single one of my neighbors knew what happened and everybody knew when I was taking a neighborhood walk, to keep an eye out to make sure I was fine. That is what got me healthy today–walking.

The Wonders of Faith

"I can do all things through him who strengthens me."
- Philippians 4:13

After a few months of walking and breathing better, one thing I kept telling myself is "I will swing my golf clubs again some day."

I put my golf clubs in one corner, put my son's picture atop of my golf clubs and kept looking at them. I knew I was going to get through this but that it would just take time. Not once during the healing time did I think about real estate. All I could think of was survival. All I could think of was, *"I wonder how God is going to use this next?"*

It took me nine months, which was the end of 2013, to get healthy. What was healthy? I was able to walk at a normal pace. I was able to relax and think to myself "What am I going to do next?" I didn't know.

"What could I do next? I didn't know that.

Will I hurt myself again?" I didn't know that either.

All I knew, without a shadow of doubt, was that none of that mattered. All I knew was that God kept me here on earth, to do something bigger and greater for Him, I just needed to figure out what and couldn't help but wonder.

The Reflection

"Whomever trust in his own mind is a fool, but he who walks in wisdom will be delivered."
- Proverbs 28:26

In the world of real estate, there is so much change. There are continual shifts in the market. As of now, there is a shift in what the industry will uphold for a REALTOR® going forward. As a REALTOR®, I can say, we are always looking at technology–

the next big thing. We can get caught up in looking at the next shiny object that we forget to look into ourselves—the talents, gifts, personalities, and capabilities we have.

I have changed greatly based upon what I have been through. It's not something I find joy in. It's not the drive I had back then as a real estate agent, or REALTOR®. Now the impact is in what I am making in people's lives, to help them to be the best they can be. It is putting a smile on someone's face, or making a memory they might hold on to forever.

I went through major seasons of change when I lived in Safford, Arizona. One was pouring my heart and soul into helping a husband and wife open up and start up an office by helping them recruit and establish their property management company. I worked diligently helping them create a strong foundation of success and have a solid start. It led to having the rug pulled out from underneath me, and I was asked to leave. Another season, another change.

At first, it was very hurtful but I now understand, even more so today, that it was a season and a part of my journey that was used to build my life today. Like being there at that time with Lupe at her brokerage, I learned a lot and God used her to help save my life. There are seasons where people are in our life: some for a moment and others for the long journey. Often, we try to hold on to something forever, when there is no forever. We grow and things evolve. Things will change and we will change, also.

Sometimes, the hardest thing is to let those changes take place because we think this is the perfect place or this is exactly where we need to be forever.

The world has influenced us. We put so much emphasis on perception, of how others see us. In addition, we layer these expectations upon ourselves with what we as humans believe we have to have. In reality, it's our choices that make these perceptions. We put pressure on ourselves, not the world.

The Journey

My life has taken a 360°. Unlike those days long ago, before my life was almost taken from me, I take time to enjoy the simple pleasures. I am not driving or pushing for the recognition. I am pushing to be true to me and if something isn't right, I have learned to be still. This allows me to hear what my body and soul are telling me.

The vulnerability to be authentic and real, the vulnerability to be heard and seen as who we are and not whom we think we should be—is priceless.

Those people who you know and who are in your life are on their own journey, as well! This is not their journey to decide for you. This is your journey! Will, it hurt sometimes? Oh my God! It will hurt. Will you be disappointed sometimes? The answer is, yes. Will you be angry at times and wonder if all this is worth it? I can assure you, wherever the journey and the path are leading you, if your heart and your soul is connected with you and you are being true to you, there will be endless opportunities to see how God is going to use you and what life is going to bring you.

By letting go, you will live life to the fullest.

Sometimes your circle grows smaller for you to be bigger. Sometimes your circle will be two or three people, instead of thirty or forty people. Know there may be a time and season that the circle will be just you, and you've got to learn to be okay with that. That transformation could be the biggest change you will experience because the hardest thing is to look at yourself.

If you have found yourself in such a place physically, spiritually or emotionally, the first thing I recommend is to read the Bible. Get in that quiet time and listen to the voice in your head. Evaluate if what it's telling you is healthy.

When you find that fear within yourself, you have to take time to stop the chaos and take time to stop the noise–just stop. It can mean getting away by yourself, listening to music, doing art, journaling or any other means by which you can escape. For me, it is love for nature and playing golf.

The purpose of sharing my story and advice is to let you know that I am going through this very thing myself. I am telling this story and am ready to have an open house for it. I thought I used to have to follow the team. But what I discovered is that God was showing me how to follow myself and let others follow alongside me, helping to build them, coaching and leading them to take the right path in each of our own journeys.

Going forward for me is to let my light shine, actually not my light–God's. It is God working through me in helping others to allow their lights shine forth. My passion lies with coaching and helping others to self-discover who they are–building their business, themselves and or families. It's left for them to discover which ever, since it's their journey, not mine. They have to freely speak into being who they really are, not what the world thinks they are to be.

To anyone who feels lost and hopeless at the moment, I will say that you matter so much more than you can possibly imagine. You owe it to yourself to look within and to be true to yourself because there "IS" a bigger plan out there.

"And Jesus said to him, 'If you can! All things are possible for one who believes.'"
- Mark 9:23

How To Build Your Faith

1. When is the last time you took time for you, quietly to rest and rejuvenate?

_____

_____

_____

_____

_____

2. Have you found yourself under stress? If so, what are some things that you are believing to cause this?

_____

_____

_____

_____

_____

3. From reading my story, knowing that I had convinced myself I had to do it all, what are you telling yourself that might be damaging your physical, emotional and spiritual well-being?

_____
_____
_____
_____

4. What are some things you need to let go of?

_____
_____
_____
_____
_____

5. What are some passions, hobbies, and experiences that need to come back in to your life? What would that do for you?

_____
_____
_____
_____
_____

6. When is the last time you had a conversation with God? Where is He, as a priority, on the relationship scale of your life?

_____

_____

_____

_____

_____

7. What have you learned from my story?

_____

_____

_____

_____

_____

About Kellie Rutherford

Her focus as a REALTOR® has always been, "The best interest of the client is the only interest to be considered." Daily she strives to provide outstanding service, ensure strong, informative communication for all stakeholders, and collaborate with a strong team that shares her vision and goals–always adding value to others.

These days, this REALTOR®-on-the-rise earns high marks from clients who as a dedicated, thorough, service-oriented, and attentive individual who blends the all-important details involved in the transaction process. One recent sales client commented: (Kellie,) "the best REALTOR® who always goes above and beyond."

Reflecting about the real estate business, Kellie finds "the relationships developed over the years and helping others" to be the most rewarding element. She adds, "helping people to fulfill their dreams of home ownership and helping them understand the home buying process, and steps along the way, gives me great joy in my business."

Kellie lives and serves in Prescott, Arizona. Professionally, she keeps abreast of new state laws and practices. Her work ethics continue to bring growth, learning, and a track record of real estate success that impacts others.

Contact Kellie

- Website: www.PrescottHasIt.com
- Email: AZKellieRutherford@gmail.com
- Phone: 928-830-0151

✝

Chapter 10

When Does God Show Up?

BY ANGELA THOMPSON

BEEP–BEEP–BEEP, usually that is all it takes is three BEEPs, and I roll over, hit dismiss, and get up. I hit the start on the coffee pot and yell to my eldest daughter to get up, in case she slept through her alarm. I grab my coffee and turn on the news to see what the weather is and see the headlines from all over the world. I often miss the weather while yelling at my middle daughter to get up and turn back to watch the tragedy around the world. PAUSE. This is my 'everyday' routine, as if the tragedy around the world, and even locally, has become so 'everyday' that I forget to instantly thank God that my family is blessed in so many ways. Have we as a society become immune or numb to the miracles that we see daily. Have you ever thought about the paths crossed and what your purpose is with people?

There are many of us that live a "normal" life with everyday routines and have opportunities to bless others that cross our paths. Do you take these opportunities, or do you look down when meeting people on the streets? Do you listen or dig for stories, or just skim the surface, not really get to know people and their hearts? This is where my real estate career has opened doors training me to listen and pray—to be present and witness to others, like yourself.

My Southern upbringing in a little Baptist Church by some pretty amazing hardworking parents has definitely helped to mold my heart into a servant one. I grew up going to church Sunday morning, Sunday evening, and Wednesday nights and attended revivals, Vacation Bible School, and anything else held at the church. Let me be clear, I didn't always want to go and griped about it often, however, my parents didn't give me a choice, and I'm so glad they were firm on my foundation. The main thing I focused on was having fun and enjoying life, and I loved art, of all kinds. I remember as a kid, waiting for my dad at the end of the fields when he was setting tobacco, or raking hay. I would sit and braid grass making necklaces and bracelets. I do believe I could be a great homesteader and live off the land.

Through school, I was often the teacher's pet and almost always a straight-A student. My cousins lived close by, and we were the best of friends, but my favorite thing to do was to spend the night at my grandparents' house watching *America's Funniest Videos* and go through Mema's photo albums hearing stories about family, and it never got old.

I was active in sports, and softball was where I felt the most comfortable. I was the pitcher—the one with the control, the Leader. I think now, softball was definitely the start of my leadership skills. I loved the pressure. I loved the control. I loved leading the rally and knowing my words and actions would impact both those on my team, and the opposing team. Have you ever compared life to sports? Looking back, it's all relative, and I'm sure as a kid, I hated the other team like they were the devil. I was there to win. I wanted to make my parents and my team proud. At that time, God was in me—I was just young and invincible—but I had not thought about making Him proud.

I graduated high school and went to a small, all girls' college in Raleigh. I had never heard of Meredith, and fully believe that was part of God's plan, as I had wanted to go to NCSU or UNC. To make a long story short, I fell in love with the Art Department and the professors, which to this day are great friends of mine. I loved the art, all of it, from drawing, to painting, to ceramic sculpture, and more. When Lisa Pierce taught me to weld, well let's just say that was another defining moment in my life. Over Christmas break of my junior year, my dad knew I had a project, and he spent the entire break working with me. He helped me find scrap metal from the woods of a local tractor repairman, "Shorty," in our county. Shorty had any old, rusted part that I could think of, and it was all out in the woods—like a scavenger hunt. Daddy had an antique, bomb-looking welder; nothing like the MIG welder I had at school. That break, he taught me to ARC weld, and together we built a life-size Egret out of metal. We had so much fun. There were so many lessons, we even talked a little about Jesus, well sorta. I still laugh when anyone talks about the "burning bush story" going back to the day in the shop when I was sitting on the concrete shop floor welding, while wearing shorts, and an arc caught my shorts burning them. Without skipping a beat, my Dad, not typically so quick-witted, laughed and said, "That was almost biblical." With a confused look, I glanced at him, and he then said, "You know, the burning bush." I didn't laugh, actually I was humiliated, but now it cracks me up. Art was my escape from the world, even though the world seemed great and pretty perfect. I loved to get into my world and create, spending time with my Dad, and hunting for old farm equipment. I wanted to give rusty old farm metal a new life;

I wanted to rescue it from rotting into nothing.

Throughout this time, I had opportunities to study abroad and do big things. Silly me had caught the love bug and couldn't bring myself to take time for me and do something super amazing like study abroad. I did agree to make a summer trip to Taos, New Mexico with the Meredith College Art Department. I had never flown, and all these other ladies were well traveled, had seen things, and it may have been exciting for them, but honestly, I felt like little Charlie when he walked into the Chocolate Factory. I got on the plane and was a bit nervous for my first flight. Even to this day when I get on a plane I have to pray: "Dear Lord, thank you so much for the blessing of being able to fly and see your beauty. I would be ever so grateful for a smooth flight that calms my nerves, and that you guide the pilots and this plane into our destination safely. Amen." Someone traded seats giving me a window seat so that I could see. I think I must have looked silly with my eyes glued out the window the entire time. I noticed over the plains and Midwest that the fields were in circles and squares and were really large compared to our little NC farm.

When we got to Albuquerque, I was taking it all in, the sky was an amazing blue, not Carolina blue, it was a vivid hue. There were very few trees, and bright orange and red canyons. There were old broken down cars on the side of the roads in the most random places that had been there 20, or more, years. We hiked the Rio Grande and Chaco Canyon. We went to the Pueblo and met amazing people with skin that was certainly that of hard-working people. Callused and wrinkled, yet a peaceful presence, very much like my grandparents. I remember looking out over Chaco Canyon and feeling so free. I could see forever, not a powerline in sight, although people were behind me and below me on trails–I couldn't see them. I truly felt the most spiritual feeling there and remember a hawk, or eagle of some kind, fly over with a huge wing-span just gliding, and I thought, "Thank you Lord for this moment." This trip did something spiritually, and artistically for me—I felt an inner peace.

Love was something I didn't miss while in New Mexico, I really was present, on an adventure. When I returned, and after school, I did marry the guy. He was great with words, had a big heart, and was a really amazing person. He, unfortunately, had demons that I could not rescue him from. As much as I tried to give, the more the demons pulled at him. I hid it from his family because of his insecurities, and I know I should have reached for help. Demons and addictions are powerful; I was influenced and did things I should not have. I know now that by God's Grace, I was able to turn my face forward and remove myself from an unhealthy marriage. I felt guilty, as no one in my family had ever divorced, and though we dated 2.5 years, our marriage was over in just six months. I felt like a failure, I felt like I was biblically wrong, and at 22 was looking to find myself. I had a great, one-bedroom apartment in Raleigh, I loved the access to downtown, and made friends at work. I had taken a job in a call-center setting appointments for health insurance agents. The pay was $10 an hour, and if I did the job well, I got to leave when I was done and was still paid for the entire day. This was a great incentive and the start of a real job for me, other than art. My skill, determination, and work ethic quickly led me to an assistant manager role, with a raise and benefits. Then I made another mistake; I began dating my boss, another unhealthy relationship. This time I knew. When I was offered another promotion, I went to the owners to explain that I had another opportunity and left, so not to ruin both of our jobs. Then, I met a Ukrainian Post-Doctoral candidate and was intrigued by him and his culture. A different religion, a different language, and culture. He was offered a position doing research at Purdue University, and you guessed it, I had to go and enrolled in Art at Purdue. I had decided I would earn a Masters degree in Art. Yep, that was my big plan. The first semester was great, I learned some Russian, and it was different–death metal, gothic parties, and a different scene than I had ever been a part of. In the underground metal scene, which I found to be very technical, artistic, I met some of the most intelligent people I have ever known and rocket scientists from around the world that understood the same language of music. I was a bit naive and gullible; I knew he was falling for me. However, I think I was just interested in the culture. I broke it off and moved home after two semesters. And although I loved Purdue, I love that when it snows in NC, everything shuts down.

You know, back in New Mexico, we would ride around the canyons in a 14-passenger van singing Dixie Chicks, and I always loved that song, *Cowboy, Take Me Away*. I think that was my fairytale in my head. So when I got back from Indiana, I was at one of my parent's friend's annual pig-pickin and went home with my childhood friend to catch up. She introduced me to her brother-in-law, and the next day we all planned to go fishing; somehow it ended up just him and me. We talked, we fished, we had a relaxing fun day, and the next day, and the next. Only three days in, I knew he was my forever. A PK (preacher's kid), bull-riding cowboy from Oklahoma. He was my cowboy and so handsome with dark brown eyes, Cherokee complexion, jeans, and boots, too. We talked all night, and he too had been married and divorced; we both had decided that it didn't matter our past and to this day, 13 years later, still don't know a lot about each other's past. I knew he was a believer and that was so very important as I wanted to have a family and wanted my kids to be brought up like me in church. We started a family soon after marriage and built a house, well, he built the house, across the field from my parents just like I had grown up across a field from my grandparents. I never thought I would be raising a family, working, and giving my kids what my parents gave me. It is such a blessing.

I took a job at a real estate office down the road doing marketing and brochures. Living paycheck-to-paycheck until one day, my broker asked me to get licensed so that he could take some weekends off and I could work office duty on the weekends. So I did. Real estate is not boring, every day is a new adventure, and you learn something. A few months in, I was doing well; the stress was high. However, I needed training and was not getting it. I found out about a larger firm that believed in God, family, and then business and trained their agents. After many tears, because I knew I was letting my broker down, I switched to Keller Williams Realty. I was in an office where people asked for prayer requests, helped one another, and cheered one another on. My first full year in real estate, 2012, I was our Rookie of the Year. I have always been competitive, and mostly with myself. I wanted to do better each year and learned about setting goals and also about serving others through my work. I have always been taught that the more you give, the more you receive, yet I think I understood that wrong as I thought it meant only monetarily. It does to some extent, however, I have come to realize that the blessings in my heart far outweigh the service.

Another defining moment in my life was when I signed up to go to KW Mega Camp in Houston, one of our national conventions, a few years ago. Ten days before the convention, Hurricane Harvey pounded on Houston leaving devastation unlike I had ever seen. Keller Williams offered refunds and saw an opportunity for our people to serve, within those ten days a huge business convention changed into an outreach and mission for RELIEF effort. I unpacked my business clothes, happily packed muck boots, mold masks, gloves, work clothes, and tools asking for my church family to pray over me. I had no clue what I was getting into and did Facebook live videos from inside the houses that showed the streets of belongings piled high as trash. My life was impacted while wheelbarrowing out soggy Bibles, family photos, teddy bears, heirlooms, and even the floors and walls to the curb. These people lost it all, yet, they were so grateful, and we prayed, we hugged, we laughed, we cried, and there was a peace that came over me and the victims I had the privilege to meet. Little did I know that these were skill sets I would use again, soon.

Back to the weather—the news said Hurricane Florence was going to be bad, and we had never seen anything like her. I have lived through hurricanes and really thought all would be fine. BEEP–BEEP–BEEP my alarm went off again as I had set it to monitor the river levels near my house. It was around 11:00 p.m. when I drove less than a quarter of a mile to the bridge and I could see the water was rising. It was raining hard, and it was dark and windy, so I really couldn't see a lot. I took my kids to my parent's home which was not surrounded by big trees, like ours, and tried to get some sleep. My husband would not come as he wanted to stay home and make sure things were okay. So, of course, I didn't sleep, and at daybreak, it was still raining. Florence had hit land, and this hurricane wasn't just crashing in on one city, this was the Carolinas, Wilmington, New Bern, and the coast was already flooding. We lost power, and I had heard that KW was heading to Wilmington to work. Well, since I had no power, my husband and team traveled with our office on Friday to de-muck in Wilmington and surrounding areas. I felt good, and my heart filled again.

On the way home from Wilmington, I learned that the river and the creek had risen and my neighbors homes were flooding. I collaborated with strangers, and we created a weekend work effort to de-muck homes, we had supplies donated, generators, laundry service, and so on. We still had no power, though we had a generator keeping the food okay. We spent the next few months getting to know the neighbors like we never had before. It wasn't about real estate; it was about praying with them, crying with them, cleaning their belongings, doing their laundry, bringing food, and showing God's love for our neighbors, showing my kids what it means to have a servant's heart.

A year later, one of the volunteers I met during this passed and one of the flood victims that I became so close with passed away. I remember both of them. Ming, a volunteer, was known locally as a servant of God and what a blessing to get to know him. Pawa lost her home to the hurricane damage and refused to leave her chickens so she and her husband lived on their porch for a couple of months until the cold came and they had to leave. She was in her 70's and so strong. She would tell me about how this was nothing compared to the tsunamis she had lived through in her country. My kids asked about her daily and wanted to check on her and her husband, bring them food, and sit and wash their belongings and wrap them up like treasures and box them away for when they were able to move.

I remember one Saturday, my kids and I along with some other volunteers got some totes, paper towels, vinegar, and water and cleaned her trinkets. It was a warm day, we were all in tees, and she was in a mechanics jumpsuit overalls and had a straw hat and work boots. Tears rolled down her cheeks as we were cleaning as she would tell stories about each little trinket. Then a praying mantis came out of nowhere, she picked it up and smiled. It was a blessing from God to her, kind of like a rainbow and she seemed okay from then on. I pray that we touched them, like they did my family and I.

I got to thinking about the little reminder of God's daily blessings, and I, too, have little reminders of special loved ones–like ladybugs remind me of my grandparents that have gone to Heaven. Even triggers of memories, such as smells and tastes, can take you back to special times. I can't help but think of how important it is to give special blessings, and memories like Christ has, to show love and mercy and live each day with a mission to make at least someone else smile. We all have opportunities daily to show God's love without having to Bible beat. I challenge each of you to think back through your life and write down memories of how God showed up. It is amazing how you may not have realized it at the time. You have moved on having not thought about it since, and then looking back now, you realize you were not alone. Little blessings–I promise, they will make your heart smile.

How To Build Your Faith

1. Have you ever thought back over time to just think of how and when God showed up?

"For I know the plans I have for you," declares the Lord, "plans to prosper you and not to harm you, plans to give you hope and a future."
- Jeremiah 29:11

_____

_____

2. I have learned to look for JOY in all things as it says here, when you are always looking for JOY even in tough times, you will find it. How has Joy kept you from looking at things differently?

Read: Philippians 1:22-30

_____
_____
_____
_____
_____

3. Have you ever had moments in time or places when all was still and you felt the presence of the Lord? How did you feel?

"We are confident, I say, and willing rather to be absent from the body, and to be present with the Lord."
- 2 Corinthians 5:8

_____
_____
_____
_____
_____

4. Do you have little reminders of lost loved ones that are in Heaven and just look up and smile?

_____

_____

_____

_____

_____

About Angela Thompson

Angela Thompson of Keller Williams Pinehurst Realty is a native of Vass, NC, just down the road. She was raised on a tobacco and chicken farm where she learned to work hard from an early age.

A graduate of Union Pines High School, Angela went on to study studio art in Raleigh at Meredith College where she graduated with a BA in fine arts and a minor in Spanish. She took a few years off to pursue her art and then went to Purdue University for graduate studies.

She loves her community and the people and with her husband of 13 + years, Kenneth, they are raising their three kids: Cecilia, Kally, and Hatch across the field from her parents. What a blessing it is to have parents nearby to help and make memories.

She is a hard worker and is often found in the community helping with charity events, her church, and spending time with her family. Her career in real estate started in 2011, and she was the Rookie of the Year her first full year in the business. She has also been selected as the local MLS as Citizen of the year and has received the Cultural award, an ALC member within her market center, and IALC (international Agent Leadership Council) representative for the Carolinas region of Keller Williams, 2018 and 2019 Best of the Pines Real Estate Agent and Property Manager.

Angela wants to help and she enjoys making it about her clients and friends and not about her. This is your journey and she is honored to help with a part of the story.

Contact Angela

- Email: Angela@AngelaThompsonGroup.com

✝

Chapter 11
Layers of Life

BY TRICIA ANDREASSEN

"There are always hidden layers within the landscape of resilience."
— Tricia Andreassen

Recently my husband and I went to the smoky mountains in Western North Carolina and Eastern Tennessee for our wedding anniversary. Every day there seemed to be a chance of rain in the afternoon and sure enough, as the weatherman predicted we did experience storms rolling through.

Here is what I found in observing the change in weather patterns dancing across the sky and melding with the mountain edges. When the clouds swooped in from above mixing with the curves and ridges of the mountains, the most beautiful views emerged. What a dichotomy to life isn't it?

For if it were clear and sunny all the time we would become bored after a while seeing the same view over and over again. In the valleys I watched the clouds dip into the crevices between the mountains, the view changed to something I could not take my eyes off of. Driving up Roan Mountain at just over 6,000 feet it was clear on the road and to the right you could see clearly for miles. The clouds mixing into the tops of the mountains and moving at a rapid pace gave such a dramatic scene you could hardly take your eyes off the shadows that were casting upon the greens. To the left you could hear remnants of thunder and see the mist of the cloud moving rapidly across the road, blanketing the view around us. Sure enough, as we made it to the top of the mountain we could hardly see our hand in front of us. The mountain midst had enveloped us where it was going to be a bit unsettling to drive out of those conditions. It gave me pause. It provided a unique perspective.

It is in our nature that although we like the certainty of things, we also crave change or variety. Of course, the double edge sword of the uncertainty can be like the weather. Sometimes interesting, bringing a unique view to an opportunity, and sometimes an all-out scary view where we have no idea what the road ahead looks like. We have all known those moments. I am in one of those right now as of this particular chapter. My 15 year old recently had shoulder surgery and it is the second time in 2 weeks we have driven from North Carolina to Michigan to deal with a sudden diagnoses of AML (Acute Myeloid Leukemia) in the family. With that said, there are many layers in life that bring vast changes in our conditions.

We have layers of our personality – complex as we are and even after many years of research the human brain much less the depth of creativity and understanding has not been fully unlocked. The mystery is there for us to explore the possibilities.

We have layers of relationships – some of the people in our life are simple and easy without much depth while others are rich, deep, and sometimes complicated. One of my close friends, Dara, shared with me a few years ago that has always resonated. She said, "Tricia, some people are to come into your life for a short period of time and some for a long time. Regardless of the time, it is meant to be as God has plans for us to learn and perhaps be in that person's life for that time to learn something." I have to say her loving and flexible comment about relationships is one of the most beautiful moments I have experienced. In the 11 years I have known her I have never heard a harsh word out of her. She has lost friends and she has gained friends and even in those changing patterns she chooses an outlook of understanding. Very much like a meteorologist who looks at the weather and recognizes the changes for what they are (while intrigued at those patterns), she has learned to be flexible to what those relationships may bring. Being 10 years younger than me she has been a phenomenal teacher in my life still today.

<u>We have layers within ourselves</u> – I imagine that all of us have said something at some particular point of, "I just don't know if I can make it through this." Perhaps it was a death of someone close to you. Perhaps it was something like a divorce where you were shaken from every bit of your core. Maybe a scenario was like a thunderstorm with a flash flood where you had several things happen at the same time and you couldn't gain your footing to save your life. Yet…Somehow you weathered through. In the midst of the storm you were in the throes of survival. And while in that, something was exposed within you that gave you the ability to hold on for the ride; to fight your way back; to hold on that this would pass and you would survive. That is why living our life reminds me of a tree growing; specifically an olive tree. You see, an Olive tree can thrive in rough terrain. It thrives with little water and in desert conditions apt to wind and rain. Yet, it is known for its resilience to the threat of fire. In its growth and resolve it takes on some of the most beautiful trunk structures that show strength and yet beauty

at the same time.

And that is not the only tree that is resilient. The palm tree lives in the most diverse areas of winds and storms and yet it does not seem to yield to those storms. Instead, it blows and it bends. Sometimes it looks like there is no way it is going to live as the leaves and fruit come crashing to the ground. But guess what? It is the storms that create the strength of the tree! It is after the storm that the trunk becomes STRONGER. It is after the effects of the weathers conditions that the trunk bends to form a beautiful shape along the waters' edge. Just close your eyes and think about it for a minute. When you think of a beautiful palm tree on this island next to the water I bet it has some type of unique bend to it.

Perhaps that is why God created such layers in all things in life. Now, don't get me wrong I am not saying that God brings those challenges necessarily. We must remember that he doesn't control our free will. I sincerely believe that he also doesn't sit up there on a throne and say "I want to give a problem to Tricia today." For I know the miraculous experiences that he provides me in the storms of what has been thrown to me. Unfortunately, we must realize that as God cast out evil in heaven that evil manifests into different scenarios of disease, depression, illness, conflict, and so much more. However what I have found in the layers of the challenge or uncertainty is when the GIFT comes; the other part of the weather that brings something beautiful to the overall picture.

As I reflect on the drive in the mountains, admiring the landscape and the trees reactions to the weather, I am reminded that it is in the cycle of life that builds our resolve and our resilience. For it is in those moments that the most beautiful blossoms emerge off those leaves. The rain creates a waterfall of beauty that would not have existed. The grass would not come back greener. The butterflies would not pond. The deer would not venture out with their young.

There would be no life. There would be no resilience to come back even stronger than before. This is why I have a meaning for each letter in the word LIFE. It creates awareness and mindfulness on how to build resilience:

LOVE - Love is talked about and it is a word used so often and yet the profound impact of love on resilience is remarkable. To be able to bounce back from the challenges life throws at us we must be able to:

Love in the possibility of what lies before us, even though we may not be able to see it. Call it hope. Call it love. To me, when things have been difficult I have been able to look at those in my life who I love and who count on me. It is in that love that responsibility and perseverance arises. The love for them I have is so strong that I must be willing to stay the course even when it seems impassible.

Love for myself, even though I am in the middle of beating myself up at the moment, the love I have for my life is stronger than the problem in front of me. The belief in me is an ingredient of love within myself. Sure I may struggle in loving some parts of me (my weight is one), but overall I love my spirit and my heart that God has given me. It is in that place that I become resilient.

1. How could you bring the feeling of self-love into your life more on a continual basis?

_____

_____

_____

_____

2. What would be some ways that you could show love to others?

_____

_____

_____

_____

_____

3. Exercise: Pretend that you are in high school or college. Imagine the perspective of the person that would have the crush on you. Write from their standpoint of why they admire you and love you so much. Yes. Write yourself a love letter. Give it to a friend or family member and have them mail it to you in six months. You will be amazed it will come at the more opportune time.

_____

_____

_____

_____

_____

INSPIRATION - When a situation looks bleak and we feel like we don't have the energy to move forward, getting inspired about something, anything, can help make it through. Perhaps you may not know it is inspiration that is happening at the moment. It could come in the humming of a song that resonates with how you are feeling. It may come in the form of writing a poem, painting a picture, or even cooking a meal for someone. I have seen it manifest through people who they are going through their own personal storm and even still they find ways to volunteer to help others in need. These are the sparks of inspiration that allow us to grab hold of optimistic viewpoints and of better moments ahead. Inspiration can create feelings of gratitude, of hope, and of contribution which all build resilience.

1. When the last time you did an activity that was considered a hobby?

_____

_____

_____

_____

_____

2. What did you love about doing it? How did you feel when you were in the process of it?

_____

_____

_____

_____

_____

3. Exercise: Think back to when you were a child. What was some of the things that you did as activities that were fun for you? For me, I realized it was singing and putting on shows in my neighborhood. In fourth grade, I wrote my own book of poems. I loved to color and paint things. It was only in this reflection that I realized these

were things that grounded me as an adult too.

Write and reflect about those moments that brought you joy. What have you realized about yourself from this exercise?

_____

_____

_____

_____

_____

FAITH - You read so much about faith in these stories. It is a core element of resilience and yet many times faith is so hard to describe. Often misconstrued as a religious word it is so much more profound. Faith is believing in something that even when the odds are stacked against you, you lean in to the knowing that all will be okay. It is a blind element that hangs in the air mixed with emotion, hope, and intuition.

1. How do you get faith?

_____

_____

_____

_____

_____

2. If this is something you struggle with, what are some things you could do that could help you build your faith? Why would that be helpful for you in your life?

_____

_____

_____

_____

_____

3. If you had more faith in your life, what could that do to your personal relationships?

_____

_____

_____

_____

_____

Your work?

_____

_____

_____

_____

_____

Your dreams?

_____

_____

_____

_____

_____

ENERGY - This is a word that isn't discussed much it seems yet it is a catalyst in every single activity in our existence. Our actions create energy. Our environment and the people we associate with create energy. We have all experience moments where we have been around certain situations where we have said "I just didn't have a good vibe" or perhaps you said "That person seems to always bring me down." It is important to remember these things when it comes to building one's resilience.

Environment contributes greatly to your mindset and the energy that feeds not only your logical mind but your spirit and soul. According to physics, energy can neither be created nor destroyed; rather, it transforms from one form to another. When you are around those who focus on negative things that will naturally transfer to you. It is a universal law of energy.

1. Who is in your life right now that brings positive energy to you in good times and bad?

_____

_____

_____

_____

2. Who could be contributing to stress in your life right now due to their transference of energy to you?

_____

_____

_____

_____

_____

3. What could you do to improve the energy around you so your mindset is resilient?

_____

_____

_____

_____

_____

4. Exercise: Go somewhere in nature that allows you to meditate and find stillness in the environment around you. What do you realize about your breathing? How does your spirit feel? What could you do to shift your energy to a state that lifts you in times of challenge?

_____

_____

_____

_____

Made in the USA
Columbia, SC
23 January 2020